CANOE COUNTRY

CAMPING

Wilderness Skills
for the Boundary Waters and Quetico

CANOE COUNTRY

CAMPING

Wilderness Skills
for the Boundary Waters and Quetico

MICHAEL FURTMAN

Illustrated by Susan Robinson

 Pfeifer-Hamilton

Pfeifer-Hamilton Publishers
1702 E Jefferson Street
Duluth MN 55812   218-728-6807

Canoe Country Camping
Wilderness Skills for the Boundary Waters and Quetico

Printed in the United States of America by Edwards Brothers Incorporated
10 9 8 7 6 5 4 3 2 1

Editorial Director: Susan Gustafson
Assistant Editor: Patrick Gross
Art Director: Joy Morgan Dey

Library of Congress Cataloging in Publication Data
92-70989

ISBN   0-938586-66-1

To those who struggle to preserve wilderness.

Table of Contents

The Boundary Waters Canoe Area Wilderness and Quetico Provincial Park

BOUNDARY WATERS CANOE AREA WILDERNESS

QUETICO

ELY

GRAND MARAIS

DULUTH

MINNESOTA

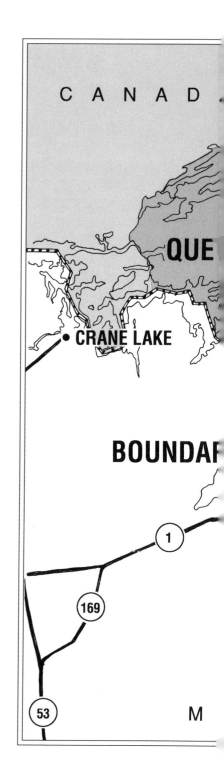

CANAD

QUE

CRANE LAKE

BOUNDAR

1

169

53

M

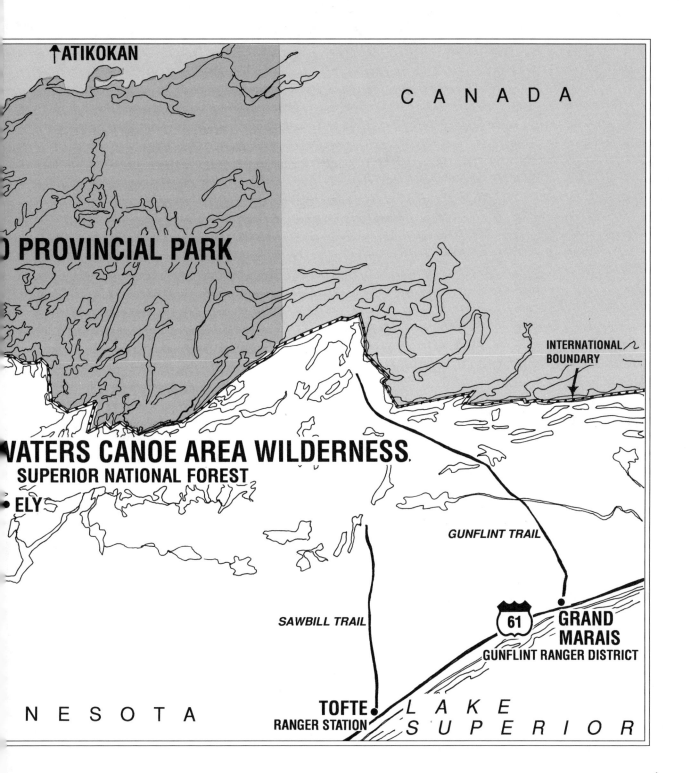

↑ATIKOKAN

C A N A D A

⊙ PROVINCIAL PARK

INTERNATIONAL
BOUNDARY

WATERS CANOE AREA WILDERNESS.
SUPERIOR NATIONAL FOREST
● ELY

GUNFLINT TRAIL

SAWBILL TRAIL

[61] **GRAND
MARAIS**
GUNFLINT RANGER DISTRICT

TOFTE ● *L A K E*
RANGER STATION *S U P E R I O R*

N E S O T A

Preface

This book, first and foremost, is about canoeing and camping skills as they are practiced in the Boundary Waters Canoe Area Wilderness of Minnesota and adjacent Quetico Provincial Park of Ontario. If you are planning a month-long run down God's River to Hudson Bay, some of the information in this book will not be useful. In fact, some of it may not even be applicable. Techniques and equipment can change with the waterway or location.

In this book I have tried to treat completely the methods and tools needed to enjoy a flatwater wilderness canoe trip in these two government-established, tightly controlled wilderness areas. Obviously, if you are canoeing in some of the similar waters elsewhere in Minnesota and Ontario, much of the book will still be appropriate. However, I wouldn't use this as a guide for canoeing the Florida Everglades.

Every book comes complete with the author's personal preferences and quirks. These biases are valuable, though, if they are the accumulated experience of the writer; they may be what qualifies him or her to write the book. Even though you may not agree with all of my suggestions, it should be some comfort to you that they come from actual experience in the field during more than a quarter of a century of canoeing. Instant experts abound these days, but I came by my experience through the old method: making repeated mistakes until I finally smartened up.

I employ the KISS method for canoe camping ("Keep It Simple, Stupid"—that "stupid" refers to me, not to you). And despite the fact that wilderness canoe tripping comes as easily to my wife, Mary Jo, and me as would walking, I have to constantly remind myself of the KISS method. We live in a gadget-filled world and some of these items seem, at the outset, wonderfully useful and just plain interesting. But time and time again, after lugging unneeded toys or using high-tech products that weren't necessary or even functional, I've had to "KISS" myself back to reality. Most of the time these things are left behind on the next trip.

That is my biggest bias: Take only what you need, and those things should be durable, uncomplicated, practical, tested, and versatile. I was a buyer and salesman for a large, well-stocked outing store. I know for a fact that much of the "new" equipment will build profits for the store and the manufacturer but isn't any better than products that have been around for quite some time. Some equipment is actually poorer than the item it purports to replace. On the other hand, it pays to embrace a new advance in equipment design or material that does improve on the old and that allows you to better enjoy the wilderness. Find that middle ground.

You will read in this book how to plan and pack for a canoe trip with minimum strain and maximum pleasure and efficiency. The advice is geared to those who wish to travel easily, and to spend more time embracing the wilderness and less time lugging things across portages. Those who can cross a portage in a single trip; can set up an efficient camp with a minimum of fuss (or fussy gear); can stay dry, warm, and comfortable; and have exercised their skills and gray matter more than their checkbook will be able to travel farther away from the wilderness's periphery. And when they do, they enhance the quality of the wilderness experience.

In the long run, skills, planning, common sense, and experience will determine the success of your canoe trip. Equipment is important to allow you to practice your skills and to keep you safe and comfortable, but you can't buy your way to a wilderness experience. In fact, the more things from the outside world you haul into the woods, the less likely it is that you will have a quality wilderness experience.

Pare your gear down. Travel lean and mean into the stony heart of the canoe country. Spend your time enraptured by wilderness, not toying with gadgets. See, feel, taste, and then finally know the true sum of your needs by stripping away the artifices and excesses of our society.

Aldo Leopold once wrote, "Recreation is valuable in proportion to the intensity of its experiences and to the degree to which it differs from and contrasts with workaday life. By these criteria, mechanized outings are at best a milk-and-water affair."

There is no one correct way to paddle a canoe or experience the wilderness. But there are definitely some wrong ways. And that is what I'll try to steer you from as you read this book. As I make recommendations, you can feel confident that they came from plenty of trial and error, doing things the wrong way as well as the right. Consider that I made your mistakes for you already. There's no reason for both of us to suffer.

Planning Your Adventure

It always surprises me that most canoe camping books place the chapter on trip planning somewhere near the end of the text. I'm not sure if this signifies how the author feels about the importance of trip-planning skills or if it is merely for organizational reasons. Whatever the reason, I've always felt such placement is erroneous.

Simply put, poor planning will equal a poor trip, every time. And this holds true no matter what your skill level. Regardless of your talents or prowess in the wilderness, you can't easily manufacture or replace most camping items forgotten at home. Nor will a poorly thought-out trip agenda or travel route be easy to modify, especially if you have only a finite number of days to complete your trip. So it behooves us to think carefully about our upcoming adventure at home and in leisure.

Not only does this make good sense, it is also good fun. After all, few of us spend as much time in the woods as we wish. Trip planning extends the adventure, increases the odds of the trip's actually meeting your expectations, and gives you the opportunity to smooth over any differences of opinion within your group before you hit the water. A few hours spent over maps and guidebooks, talking about your expectations and checking the gear and food list, both is a pleasure and makes good sense.

Poor Planning = Poor Trip

Trip planning is fun, extends the adventure, and makes good sense

**Careful planning
will give you**

❑ More free time

❑ Confidence

❑ Personal comfort

❑ Safety

**Take a good look at your
paddling partners**

Are they all in good shape?

Do they have good canoeing
and camping skills?

So what's the big deal, you ask? This is supposed to be an adventure, isn't it? We're going to the Boundary Waters and Quetico to experience freedom, aren't we? Absolutely. In fact, the one thing I hate most on a canoe trip is having to adhere to a rigid agenda. Such rigidity places constraints on me that I have little tolerance for, especially on a canoe trip. But that is not what we are talking about here.

By taking time before the trip to do some careful planning, you will actually increase your free time and freedom because you won't have to try to compensate for errors in judgment or failures in equipment. You'll feel confident that whatever arises, you'll be able to handle it. You'll know your equipment is up to each test. And you'll be able to concentrate on doing those things you go to the canoe country to do: read, explore, fish, or photograph. This is where planning pays off.

Planning pays dividends in personal comfort and safety as well. Being wet or cold, too tired or too hungry, bug-bitten or lost—all come from being unprepared and add nothing but misery to a canoe trip. Avoiding these things only takes a modicum of skill but it does require good sense and forethought.

Planning only becomes complicated when we factor in skill levels. For skills will, to a large measure, determine not only how you plan but exactly what you plan. For instance, if you carry lots of gear, need to make multiple trips across portages, and are a little rusty with paddle skills or a bit out of shape (let's be honest here, folks), you need to modify your trip plan to take these things into consideration.

An example might be a simple canoe trip heading north from Kawishiwi Lake near the Sawbill Trail. Because of the way we pack and portage, I know that Mary Jo and I can get to Malberg Lake in an easy four hours. However, if we had to make multiple trips on the portages, Lake Polly might be as far as we could get before getting tuckered out. We wouldn't reach Malberg until the second day. Knowing your limits is critical to planning a trip.

Equally important is assessing the reason for your trip. Are you interested in doing a lot of fishing? Do you intend to visit a pictograph site? Is solitude more important than ease of access? Obviously, in that first example, if fishing were my first concern, we wouldn't have pushed on quickly to Malberg Lake but would have dallied and enjoyed some of the fine fishing along the way. If you have a diehard angler in your group, you'll need to allow time or you'll have one very unhappy camper.

Similarly, in order to visit the pictograph site on the Kawishiwi River to the west of Malberg, fast, light travel would be a necessity. Consider that most visitors to the BWCAW spend only four days on a canoe trip; in Quetico it is five. Reaching these fascinating rock paintings would take most folks two days when entering from Kawishiwi Lake; hence a full four-day canoe trip would be consumed, round trip.

Should solitude be your primary reason for visiting the canoe country, you need to plan accordingly. Had that been our goal, we likely would not have found it on Lake Polly, at least during the busiest part of the summer. But by scrutinizing our maps before leaving home, no doubt we would have set our sights on a small lake off the main travel route, preferably one with a single campsite.

It should come as no surprise then that many factors will influence your trip plan. We'll cover packing, portaging, and paddling skills later. Initially, though, you'll have to rank your capabilities in these areas while planning. Equipment choices can also influence your route plan or length, and these we'll cover in detail.

Even rules and regulations will determine much. Consider that in the BWCAW you must camp at a designated campsite. What happens if the lake you reach at the same

What are your goals for the trip?

❏ Fishing?

❏ Photography?

❏ Solitude?

❏ Sightseeing?

Pictograph

3

time as the limit of your energy has no designated campsite, or none that are empty? Camping illegally will result in a stiff fine; poor planning is not an excuse that is likely to sit well with the ranger or magistrate. Had you had some good idea how far you could travel in a day, you might have avoided ending up pooped out at a lake with no sites. Careful planning would have meant you'd know where the next likely unoccupied campsite might be.

Had your trip been to the Quetico, where camping anywhere is allowed, you might have trusted your luck to find a likely looking campsite wherever and whenever you decided to quit for the day. We often do this and it is totally acceptable—but not in the BWCAW.

Consider also, when planning, the size of the lakes and frequency and length of portages. Big lakes can mean easy travel, perhaps as far as twenty or more miles per day. The risk, however, is wind. Not taking into account that wind may slow or stop you is foolish, maybe even dangerous. Small lakes mean many portages. Even short portages take time. The slowest part of portaging for many, especially those whose gear is not well organized, is loading and unloading at landings.

Finally, consider the abilities of those in your party. You will travel only as fast as the slowest in your group. If you are traveling with small children, realize that you'll not be able to travel nearly as far or as fast as you would in an adults-only group. Canoe trips that include children should be tailored for their needs, and more ambitious adventures should be saved for another time. Kids can do very well in the canoe country, but you'll need to scale back your plans. The same is true, really, if you have inexperienced adults in your group. Never plan a route more difficult than the slowest and least able in your party can handle.

It is clear that good planning is a balancing act where one juggles those things that we know (equipment weight and

How fast can you go?

You are only as fast as the slowest member of your group

type, paddling and portaging skills, number and length of portages) against those things that remain unknown (weather, portages blocked by blowdowns, low water in rivers, difficulty in locating a campsite). Toss in your ultimate purpose for the trip (solitude, fishing, etc.) and you begin to see that all factors are interactive.

In the end, much will be determined by just how hard you are willing to work. Let's admit it. Most of us aren't used to this kind of physical exertion. Four or five hours of it may be more than enough. So while theoretically an eight-hour day might put you at the lake of your dreams, if you are ready to throw in the towel after four hours, why not plan on it? You'll not be disappointed because you couldn't reach an unattainable goal and you'll enjoy the trip that much more because you won't be aching or exhausted.

But we must begin somewhere. First decide on your objectives for this canoe trip. Most likely it will include a little sightseeing, some fishing, and perhaps a layover day to just plain relax. You are driving some distance to reach the canoe country so your first and last days on the water will not be full ones; you will have to drive for a few hours during each of these days. Within the remaining days you must squeeze this precious adventure.

Select an entry point

Choosing an entry point for your trip takes some thought. You may choose to go via entry points near Ely, Grand Marais, Sawbill, or Atikokan. Good outfitting services are located near or in all these locales. The only way you can decide where to go is also to decide why you're going, and then pore over maps of the area. Both the Quetico and Boundary Waters entry points are ranked by the governing agencies by popularity and by the number of permits available per day. I can guarantee you that those routes that are the easiest are also the most popular, and hence have more permits available. If solitude is

The known

❑ Equipment

❑ Skills

❑ Length of portages

The unknown

❑ Weather

❑ Condition of portages

❑ Availability of campsites

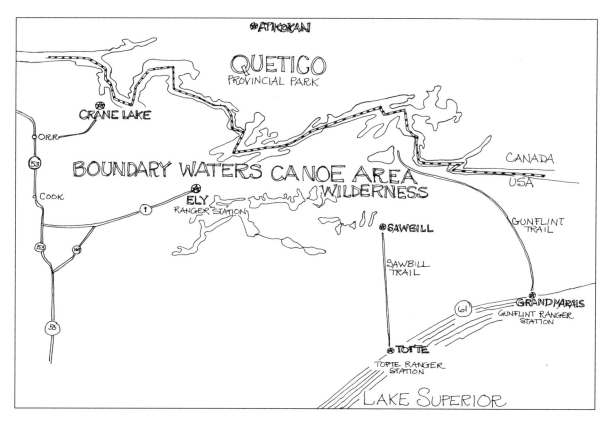

Lily pads can choke streams

what you crave, you may not like these routes unless you seek seldom-used lakes that are off these travel corridors.

Other factors to consider when choosing an entry point might be the size of the lakes, length or frequency of portages, and whether there are many miles of river travel. Keep in mind that many of the canoe country's small streams get low or weed-choked in late summer, making traveling them challenging. Guide books, such as those written by Robert Beymer, can help you make a decision. If fishing is your forte, and you want to know what kind of fish are in the lakes you'll visit, you'll want to purchase my book, *A Boundary Waters Fishing Guide,* which has the only complete lake index to both the Quetico and Boundary Waters, as well as in-depth information on equipment and fishing techniques.

Plan your route

For whatever reason, perhaps even arbitrarily, you've chosen a particular entry point to the BWCAW or Quetico. Beyond that entry point lies the wilderness. On your map it is a wonderful, mysterious maze of water and forest, stitched together by the dotted lines of portages. The routes are many, the choices confusing. Where to go?

Knowing your personal objective helps. Now you must determine the speed at which you can travel. That will be determined by how you pack and how you paddle (aside from difficulties such as poor weather). Frequency and length of portages will also play a role.

Start by studying the map and consulting guide books if you wish (see suggested reading list). Count the number of portages and total their length. Most canoe country maps measure portages in rods. One rod equals sixteen feet. A mile equals 330 rods. Approximate the total water miles as well. Now you have an idea of what lies before you.

Good paddlers in swift canoes can keep a steady five-mile-per hour pace for many hours. Most of us won't be able to do that. A good rule of thumb would be three miles per hour. If you have packed lightly so that portages fall to a single trip, a mile portage will take only twenty minutes. If you have to double portage it will take three times that long. (The reason a "double" portage triples the time is that you must actually traverse the trail three times: twice with gear, once to go back and get the second load.)

How fast can you paddle?

5 mph: strong paddlers in good conditions

3-4 mph: average

1-2 mph: out-of-shape paddlers or poor conditions

Estimate your travel time

Now you can begin to estimate your travel time. For each mile *– At least!* of portaging making multiple trips figure on one hour. For each mile of water, figure twenty minutes. If you have many portages, but they are short, the load and unload time begins

**A long first day of travel—
perhaps too long and tiring**

5.0 hours	drive to entry
2.5 hours	paddling
1.5 hours	portaging
.5 hours	loading
.5 hours	lunch
.5 hours	breaks
10.5 hours	TOTAL

to add up. Figure in an additional five to ten minutes for each portage. Now toss in a nice long lunch break, a few snack breaks (one per hour if you are really laboring), and a little time for leisure.

Let's say you've got your heart set on feeling the breeze from a particularly sun-kissed point on Lake X. This lake is the sixth lake in a chain beginning at your chosen entry point. The first lake is three miles long, the other four barely a mile long apiece. The portages vary from very short to fairly long but total 450 rods (330 rods per mile).

The seven miles of water will take two hours and twenty minutes to paddle at our hypothetical three miles per hour. Four hundred and fifty rods of portages, making multiple trips, will require an hour and a half. Toss in at least another half hour for loading and unloading and yet another thirty minutes for snack breaks.

Somewhere along the way you'll want a real rest so add in another thirty minutes for lunch. Total time to Lake X will be almost five and a half hours. If you had to drive until noon to get to the landing, this might be too much to do the first day—or on the last day, with the drive home. I've found this means of estimating canoe country travel time to be pretty accurate. But if you arrive at Lake X at midnight, please don't blame me.

While we'll be talking more about the details of the single portage later, it is interesting to note in this example that if you could have crossed the portages each in a single trip, you would have axed at least an hour and a half from your travel time—something definitely worth thinking about. Polish your paddling skills so you can hit five miles per hour and suddenly you lop off another hour. Practice not only makes perfect, it seems, but makes life easier as well.

When I talk about saving time, don't confuse it with being in a rush. I'm the most unrushable person there is. What I'm referring to throughout this book is actually taking things easier and with more leisure. After all, I'm sure we can both think of better ways of spending our time on a canoe trip than portaging. That extra hour saved may be the hour you wanted to try to get a photo of a moose, listen to the loons, or catch a plump walleye.

Maps are important

Good maps are a crucial element to planning any canoe trip. Fortunately for us, there are wonderful maps available for those wishing to explore the Quetico and BWCAW. Fisher Map Company, of Virginia, Minnesota, has an excellent set of maps called the F series that strikes the best compromise of scale: small enough so that each map covers a fair-sized swath of the canoe country, large enough so that topographic details remain clear. Make sure your maps are current. Frequently the Forest Service reviews maps of the BWCAW for accuracy, and the date of that revision is usually located on the map's bottom margin. Of most importance are portage and campsite locations. Yes, these things do change occasionally. If a campsite has been closed because of fire or wind damage or overuse, you want to know that before your trip, not when you arrive at that former campsite.

Should you have questions about your route, the time to ask them is before you set out. Your outfitter, if you use one, can be immensely helpful. So too can the Quetico and BWCAW rangers. Direct your questions to the ranger station nearest your entry point. They'll be much more likely to be familiar with the particulars of your route.

Checklists are invaluable for ensuring that items have not been left behind. We'll address these more in the equipment chapter. Just make sure you use one.

Remember, if all of this seems only too obvious it is also too important to neglect. The foundation of a successful canoe country visit is laid at home, with a map, pencil, and checklists. No trip ever suffered from too much planning. Plenty have gone awry for lack of it.

No trip ever suffered from too much planning

9

Travel time

Water	3 miles/hour
Single portage	3 miles/hour
Double portage	1 mile/hour

Portages are measured in rods

One rod = 16 feet

One mile = 5,280 feet

One mile = 330 rods

For city folk

Think of those portages in terms of a familiar distance for walkers. There are 27.5 rods in a city block.

When the sun presses warm on your face and the breeze cools your pleasantly sweaty neck, when tufts of white clouds ride quickly on the blue sky's breeze and you hear the lapping of waters on the hull of your canoe, you can sit back and relax. You know that in those weathered green Duluth Packs resides all the equipment and food you'll need and that nothing was forgotten. You know how far you've come and how far you can expect to get yet this day. The whole of the majestic canoe country lies awaiting your explorations.

Just the way you planned it.

How many hours from here to there?

The most frequently asked question I receive (next to inquiries on fishing, anyway) is "Do you think we can get into that lake in a day?" Obviously, many people share the inability to estimate their travel capabilities.

This chapter covers in detail how to estimate travel time in the canoe country, but so that you don't have to go back and hunt up the formulas, here they are without the explanations. First, total all the portage lengths and separately compute your water miles along the route to your intended goal, then use the chart on the next page to compute your travel time. Your result will not include rest breaks or loading/unloading time, and it won't reflect the effects of high winds or portage ruggedness, so allow extra time. Study your topographic maps to determine if portages are likely to have much vertical and then plan for extra rest periods.

Finally, parallel routes to the same destination might exist, and usually they consist of one route with few long portages mirroring another route with short frequent carries. Believe it or not, if the total amount of rods to be portaged is about the same for the two, the route with the few long carries might be faster, but only if you single portage. The frequent landings and time spent unloading and loading on the other route can eat up time.

Travel Time Worksheet

Water travel	# of miles	_____ ÷ 3	= hours on water	_____
If single portaging	# of rods	_____ ÷ 990	= hours on portages	_____
or				
If double portaging	# of rods	_____ ÷ 330	= hours on portages	_____
Loading and unloading canoe				_____
Rest breaks				_____
	Estimate of total travel time			_____

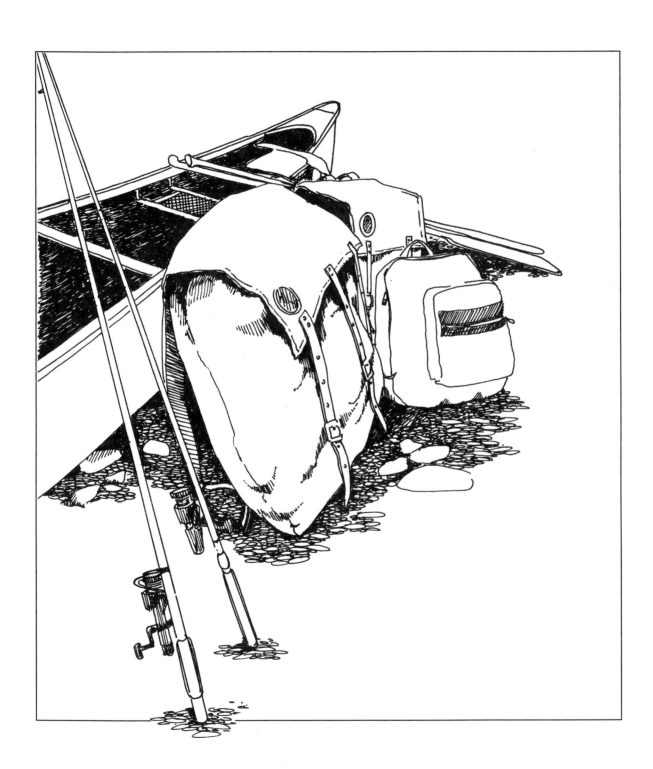

Good Gear = Good Trip

I awoke early in the morning after a night of fitful thunder-boom interrupted sleep, dressed, and leaving the Crooked Lake cabin, the little log building where Mary Jo and I were stationed as wilderness rangers during the summer of 1986, stepped outside into the soggy morning. The night had been one of ferocious thunderstorms and driving rains. Windrows of pine needles and other floating debris lined the lake's shoreline as evidence of the deluge that had only just ended.

Surveying the storm damage, I strolled into one of the two campsites within a short walk of the cabin. A young married couple stood forlornly around a smoldering fire, trying vainly to warm themselves. The woman shuddered involuntarily.

Their belongings hung everywhere in camp, strewn on every dripping branch. Sleeping bags, clothing, and personal items draped damply. I helped them bring their fire to a blaze; while I did, I saw the reason for their misery. Standing in a pool of water was the most miserable excuse for a tent I had ever seen, a cheap, poorly designed hunk of nylon that some manufacturer actually had the gall to sell for the intended use of camping.

It is fortunate that the canoe country is a benevolent wilderness. Few people who experience its worst, at least in

Bad gear = Bad trip

All that may stand between you and an enjoyable trip is poor equipment.

the summer, come away from the ordeal with anything worse than a case of the shivers. Those who experience that, however, are quite numerous. Unfortunate, because often all that stood between them and an enjoyable trip was their equipment choice. Bad equipment = bad trip. Guaranteed.

Perhaps this young couple had chosen that tent because it was all they could afford. I sympathize with anyone who wants to experience the canoe country but simply can't afford to purchase expensive gear. But in this case they would have been much better off renting a tent from an outfitter, a tent that would do what a tent is intended to do—protect them from the elements.

Good equipment need not be expensive

At the other end of the spectrum from this young couple are camping gear techno-crazies, folks who purchase fancy equipment that often performs only marginally better, and sometimes worse, than more moderately priced but well-designed products.

I have a simple philosophy when it comes to new "improved" products. First, they must be as simple as those tried-and-true items they are supposed to replace. Complexity of design has no place in the wilderness and leads to irritation and product failure. Second, they must be as durable as previous products. Why pay more for something that will fail sooner? Last, they must perform at least as well as older designs. I will suffer with slightly diminished performance only if the new item is significantly better in some other category, such as weight or durability.

Using these criteria I find many trendy camping products just that: trendy. Because I am fortunate enough to write about such things for a living, I am able to field-test many items and can evaluate them without the expense of purchasing them. Time and time again, I have returned to my old standby equipment after using the latest high-tech

New and improved products

❏ Must be as simple as the tried-and-true original

❏ Must be as durable as the original

❏ Must perform as well as the original

❏ Must be field-tested

14

stuff. And the major reason for this is that the new gear didn't live up to inflated claims; if there was some improvement, it came at enormous increased expense or gear "fussiness," requiring innumerable adjustments and endless fiddling around.

That doesn't mean that all new gear and technologies are bad. Quite the contrary. We have fantastic equipment to choose from, things only dreamed of decades ago. But the key is to look for items that have been tested, that have been on the market long enough to show failures in design and to have been improved. I don't like being a guinea pig. I have often wondered, for instance, if some tent makers have ever actually slept in their products during a long downpour. Having used sophisticated, extremely expensive tents that leak, not because of incidental manufacturing defects but because of basic poor design, I suspect that little field testing was done before marketing the products.

Plan carefully before you buy

There is, however, much good equipment to choose from— so much so that choices can be bewildering. Since you won't have the luxury of testing a product before purchasing it, it is important to be sure of exactly what you want before whipping out your checkbook.

As in planning a canoe trip, buying equipment begins with a kind of holistic approach. You must determine every criterion of a product before the purchase. If you select a tent solely on its shape, but do not consider its weight and packing size, you may find it a terrible nuisance to pack and carry. Sleeping bags that meet your temperature requirements but won't stuff down to a size suitable to fit in anything less than half a Duluth Pack are similarly a poor choice. A tiny super-light stove that requires intricate assembly each time it is used inevitably ends up missing an important part. And so on.

Your particular requirements are far more important than any advertising claims or the recommendations of your canoeing friend. For instance, if your friend prefers to make multiple trips on portages, never travels great distances, and only base camps, his or her fourteen-pound tent recommendation will be a curse if you plan on single portaging and traveling light. It is almost critical that you decide at the outset whether you will be striving to single portage most of the time and therefore must pack light. For not only will equipment choice determine your comfort, it will determine how you pack. And how you pack will determine how you travel and how fast you travel. It is important that you keep this in mind as you examine your equipment choices.

While there is a lot of leeway in your final selection, your major equipment needs will be constant. Let's take a look at critical criteria for each category.

Your tent—a home in the wilderness

A tent has one major function: to protect you from the elements. Amazingly, many tents, including some expensive models, don't do this very well.

But along with providing protection from wind, rain, and insects, a tent must also be durable, simple to erect, roomy, and of a size and weight that makes packing easy. You must also be able to afford it.

Almost all tents today are made of nylon, a fabric that combines both durability and light weight. Waterproof portions such as bathtub floors and the rain fly are generally of urethane-coated nylon. Until some other fabric comes along that is more suitable, restrict your choice to a nylon tent.

Features important to a good tent are a separate rain fly (to allow moisture within the tent to escape through the breathable inner wall) that extends down nearly to the ground, no-see-um-proof netting on doors and windows, adequate ventilation even when most apertures are zipped up against a

A good tent is

- ❏ Wind proof
- ❏ Rain proof
- ❏ Insect proof
- ❏ Durable
- ❏ Simple to erect
- ❏ Roomy
- ❏ Lightweight
- ❏ Affordable

Overhanging eaves

wind-driven rain, a sewn-in bathtub floor that extends well up the side walls (at the very least, a couple inches above the overlap with the rain fly), and a good weight-to-space ratio.

Most quality tents will meet these requirements. Stay away from models that have waterproof walls with no, or a very small top-of-the-tent, rain fly. Look for tents with aluminum poles, preferably of aircraft grade. Watch out for tents where the main source of ventilation is a door that slants backward. In a rain, when you need ventilation the most, you can't open that kind of door to provide a draft without allowing in precipitation. And with any tent, the fewer the seams on critical waterproof areas, such as the floor and rain fly, the better. While seam sealant is necessary on all sewn seams to provide maximum protection from water, seam sealant does wear out, sometimes at a most inopportune time. The fewer the seams, the less the odds of any problem.

If you have ever been forced into a tent for hours during rains, or needed to escape from particularly ferocious hordes of biting bugs, you know the need for adequate interior space. Finding a tent with plenty of room at a reasonable weight can become a quest.

Most two-person tents have about forty square feet of space. While this is adequate for sleeping, it provides virtually no room for gear storage and can be claustrophobic during prolonged periods of confinement. The most attractive thing about two-person tents is their weight. The majority weigh between five and seven pounds.

Four-person tents offer up to sixty square feet of living space. Such tents, provided they are reasonably light, really are a better choice for two or three people. You can while away the hours in comfort, there is less build-up of condensation, and some water-sensitive gear, such as extra clothing, cameras, and the like, can be stored indoors. The major failing of these tents is weight. Some tip the scale at over ten

Bathtub floor

Characteristics of a good tent

- ❏ Nylon fabric
- ❏ Separate rain fly
- ❏ Fine mesh netting
- ❏ Sewn-in bathtub floor
- ❏ Aircraft grade aluminum poles
- ❏ Good ventilation
- ❏ Few sewn seams

Tent and pole bags

pounds—some as high as fourteen. An ideal four-person tent weighs nine pounds. Such a weight will allow you to keep your gear pack in that magic twenty-five to thirty pound range that allows for single portaging.

A category that is often overlooked because there are fewer tent offerings within it is that of the three-person tent. I consider a three-person tent one that provides a minimum of forty-eight square feet of interior space (watch out—some tent manufacturers include exterior vestibule space in their square-foot ratings). These tents are ideal for two people, because they provide luxurious interior space and often weigh around seven or eight pounds.

The problem with vestibules is that they don't provide truly waterproof protection for gear (most have no floor and rainwater can run beneath them) and the addition of one to a two-person tent quickly puts it in the weight range of a three- or light four-person tent without contributing anything to livable interior space. With a three- or four-person tent, the added room just won't be necessary when the tent is used by two or three people.

A great many tents are self-supporting (sometimes called freestanding), meaning it is not absolutely necessary to stake them down. This is deceiving. Even self-supporting tents

Lightweight but roomy—the tent trade-off			
	2-person	3-person	4-person
Floor space	40 sq. ft.	48 sq. ft.	60 sq. ft
Weight	5-7 lb.	7-8 lb.	9-14 lb
Comfortably accomodates	1-2	2	2-3

require staking in a wind. And if a tent is to offer good protection in a rain, it must be drawn very tight. A sagging tent will collect water in slack fabric pockets, or the rain fly will gap, allowing in wind-driven rain. Additionally, tents not drawn tightly will allow the rain fly to sag and contact the interior, nonwaterproof wall. A great deal of moisture condenses on the inside of a rain fly and when this contacts the actual tent wall, it will surely drip into the tent. I'd bet most "leaky" tents really don't leak at all, but suffer from either a poor design that allows such contact or haven't been drawn tightly enough.

Freestanding tents then really do need to be staked down in order to provide the protection for which you carry a tent. Although freestanding tents are convenient, they are not necessary, even in the shallow-soil canoe country. In fact, to stake one of these tents down often requires as many stakes as with a nonfreestanding model. Consider this feature a nicety rather than a necessity. Since freestanding or self-supporting tents require more poles than other types, you often pay a price in added weight for a feature that is largely unneeded. Lightweight aluminum skewer-type tent stakes are easier to use in this region's rocky soil and take up less space in the pack than more traditionally sized tent pegs.

Style is another debatable subject. The best tents are usually either A-frame or dome-like in design. Domes offer nearly vertical walls, thus better using interior space, especially for sitting up near those walls. But they are often heavier because of all the poles. A-frames are cheaper and simpler to erect. Both are more than adequate for the type of wind and weather you'll encounter in the BWCAW or Quetico. Let your pocketbook and personal taste guide your choice.

Suppose you've found two tents that seem to meet your general needs and are similarly priced. How do you choose? Consider the fine points now. A rain fly that has adjustable

Skewer-type tent stake

Tent styles

- ❏ A-frame
  lighter
  cheaper
  easy to erect
  less interior space

- ❏ Dome
  heavier
  more expensive
  more difficult to erect
  more interior space

19

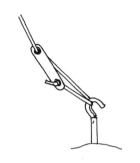

Adjustable stake-out loops

Features you'll appreciate

❑ Adjustable stake-out loops on the rain fly

❑ Tape-sealed seams

❑ Fly with large overhang

❑ Roof vents

❑ Mesh pockets

❑ Anodized aluminum poles that break into short lengths

Aluminum tent poles

stake-out loops, as opposed to shock cords, should get the nod. Nylon sags when wet, and shock cords do an inadequate job of keeping the fly taut. To protect you best from the worst of storms, a fly should be drawn as tight as a drum while dry. It is only going to get looser as it gets wet during the storm.

Examine the number of seams in the fly and floor. The fewer the better. If they are factory tape-sealed, great. Take a look at how much of an overhang the fly provides above doors and windows. The more the better. Roof vents are nice for added ventilation. Mesh pockets sewn inside provide safe storage for small items. Aluminum poles are stronger and lighter than fiberglass; high-grade aluminum (usually anodized gold or black) is stronger and lighter than the lower grade (usually silver colored). Two doors, rather than one door and one window, also add convenience.

One last criterion to consider. Since most lightweight tents are designed for the backpacking market, and since most backpacks are much taller than canoe packs, tent poles often break down into thirty-inch lengths. Not a big deal if you're putting them down the length of a long backpack, but a big deal if you are trying to squeeze thirty inches into a twenty-eight-inch canoe pack (which is a common size). Sure, you can let them stick out above the top flap, or place them under the flap and across the pack's width, but I can assure you that you'll end up snagging the poles on just about everything each time you load and unload the canoe, try to wear the pack while portaging the canoe, or have to bushwhack on a seldom-used portage. If you can find a tent with poles in the twenty to twenty-six inch range, you'll be much happier.

Such fine points should help narrow the choice even further. Once it's purchased, set the tent up at home and seal all the fly and floor seams that may ever be exposed to moisture. Then seal them again!

An ideal canoe country tent for two people would weigh

about seven or eight pounds while providing about fifty square feet of space. It would set up simply, withstand high winds, have an almost-to-the-ground rainfly with adjustable tension, come with two doors and a roof vent, and have aircraft-quality aluminum poles that break down into two-foot lengths.

I've seen and used a lot of tents in my time. Some were pretty high-tech. But the measurement against which each must stand has remained the same. If it doesn't keep the elements out while keeping me happy within, it isn't worth a dime.

A typical canoe country tent

Canoe packs

Packs for canoe camping are special in that one of their most important functions has nothing to do with being carried. In fact, a canoe pack sits more than it is worn, so the emphasis is on how it fits in a canoe and how it affects a canoe's center of gravity. And when the pack is worn, it must ride below the shoulders so the wearer can simultaneously carry a canoe. These features distinguish canoe packs from either an internal or an external frame backpack.

Backpacks are not suitable for canoe camping. They don't fit well in a canoe because of their protruding frames and their length. Standing upright in your canoe, they rise far above the gunwale, creating a very poor center of gravity. Because they extend above your shoulders when worn, you can't wear one and portage a canoe at the same time. Since most have many compartments, they are impossible to waterproof with a single liner bag. Yes, they do carry loads better than a canoe pack; but remember, carrying loads is only half of a canoe pack's job.

Since Camille Poirier patented the design for the first canoe pack in 1892, the basic design and function haven't changed much. Known initially as the Poirier pack, and

A canoe pack sits in the bottom of the canoe more than it rides on your back

since then as the venerable Duluth Pack, they have stalwartly met the needs of canoeists for generations.

The Duluth Pack, which is built only by Duluth Tent and Awning of Duluth, Minnesota, has been the standard for a century now, and all newcomers to this category of packs copy the Duluth Pack to some degree. Some even claim to have improved upon it, although in my experience, those claims fall short. The term *Duluth Pack* has become almost generic, as has the original method of measuring canoe packs by the numbers 2, 3, and 4, referring to their size. In reality, Duluth Pack is a trade name registered by Duluth Tent and Awning. The original Duluth Pack, and all its imitations, do two things that a backpack doesn't: ride low in the canoe and sit below shoulder height so the pack can be worn while carrying a canoe.

How important are these points? Well, if you can't carry the pack and the canoe at the same time, you'll seriously limit your flexibility when portaging. You'll never be able to single portage if you can't carry both, and so your time on portages will be increased by a factor of three every time.

Duluth Packs are also soft, allowing them to assume the contours of a canoe. If at all possible, none of your load should project above the gunwales of the canoe. Duluth Packs lie flat and snug in the round confines of a canoe, and unless they are of the box type, they'll even squeeze underneath yokes and thwarts. Even when placed standing up in a canoe, Duluth Packs still provide a low center of gravity.

Many genuine Duluth Packs come complete with a tumpline, a wide strap that rises from the top of the pack to snug down across the top of a portager's head. Indians and voyageurs relied solely upon tumplines for carrying heavy loads, using the advantage of strong neck muscles and the fact that placed correctly, the tumpline positions load weight directly on the wearer's center of gravity. Most canoeists today no longer use a tumpline, which is a shame. Some

A canoe pack should

- ❑ Ride low in the canoe
- ❑ Sit below shoulder height when on your back

#3 Duluth Pack

have found it painful, mistakenly wearing the tumpline on the forehead, causing severe neck strain. To be effective, the tumpline should be worn across the top of the head, just behind the forehead. Pulling down on the tumpline, one hand on each side of the neck, centers the load and makes the system work.

A number of canoe packs are available now, from the tried-and-true canvas and leather original Duluth Pack to an array of nylon high-tech models. I've used most of them and all worked well. But that doesn't mean I think they're all equal. My personal choice is the #3 Duluth Pack. The Duluth Pack comes as near to a perfect canoe pack as any ever created, and no other pack rides as well in the canoe or looks as good in the woods.

The most "sophisticated" new packs sport padded shoulder straps, sternum straps, hip belts, and elaborate top-closure systems. Most are made of Cordura or ballistic-cloth nylon. Some are literally festooned with D rings and compression straps. All of these packs come with hefty price tags. And most sport features unnecessary for canoeing the Quetico and BWCAW, where the longest portages are only a mile and many are merely short "liftovers."

The biggest problem I have with these "new-fangled" packs is the great extremes to which they go to keep water out of the top closure. These ingenious tops roll down, fold over, zip shut, hook-and-loop together, strap down, and buckle together, all in an effort to stop water from entering the pack. But the only thing they keep out of the pack is you! This irritation is doubly maddening because these packs aren't waterproof anyway. Believe me, I've tested them all in controlled experiments, and each one leaks. So what good is a watertight closure system that will prevent you from easily and quickly retrieving your camera or rain gear while straining and reaching in a floating canoe, when most of the water the pack takes on will be through the multitude of seams

Frame style packs

❏ Are comfortable to carry

❏ Tend to be leaky

❏ Interfere with carrying canoes

❏ Are relatively expensive

sewn through the pack material? A few pack manufacturers recommend that these packs be placed flap side down in the canoe, to minimize water infiltration through the hip and shoulder straps' numerous seams. This means that in order to get into your pack while you are in the canoe, not only must you struggle with all the closures at the top, but first you have to turn the thing over. Sure. Go ahead. But don't try doing it on anything but flat water, or bother to haul out rain gear in a quick rain squall, or expect that big bull moose to hold his majestic pose while you try to get at your camera.

There is one good point to these packs. They are comfortable to carry. The hip belt helps to distribute weight to the strong leg muscles and to eliminate strain on the shoulders. But considering that they are two to three times the cost of a traditional-style canoe pack, are no more waterproof (we'll cover waterproofing in the packing chapter), and have a lot more bells and whistles that get hung up on everything or get torn off, I have a hard time getting too enthusiastic about them. This type of pack might be a good choice for a food pack, because you get into the food pack only infrequently during the day and the hip belt helps with food's weight. Then again, watching a black bear slash it to ribbons or play fullback with it and make for the forest endzone might make me think twice, considering these packs' price tags.

Although a lot of packs are now being made of nylon, don't let this material's popularity convince you that it is always a better choice than heavy canvas. In fact the only canoe pack I've ever worn a hole in on a single trip (granted, it was a month-long trip) was a Cordura nylon model. On the other hand, I have twenty-five-year-old canvas models that are still going strong. For even though laboratory tests show nylon holds up better to abrasion, these tests ignore one simple point. Canvas gives and stretches; nylon packcloth doesn't. Dropped and dragged across the canoe country's abrasive granite, cotton canvas gives, but nylon puts up a fight. Like a tree that bends to a wind, the canvas survives. And like the rigid tree that snaps in the gust, nylon has been known to wear right through.

What I'm saying is that either material will give you suitable wear, but don't sell canvas short because of its "low-tech" status. I find that canvas's soft warmth and graceful weathering are its best qualities, especially when compared to the petroleum-derived, trendy-colored nylon packs.

Some canoe packs available today are simply enlarged versions of "dry bags" with attached shoulder straps. These packs are truly waterproof and so at first glance would seem an ideal choice. Constructed of heavy waterproof PVC-coated nylon material with welded seems, they allow in no water. Their failings are the plasticized material, which doesn't hold up well to the stony tests of the canoe country, and their height of over thirty inches, putting them in that too-long-to-wear-when-portaging-a-canoe category. For river trips they are great, however.

I think it's unfortunate that most canoe pack designs have gone to a box styling. Canoe packs come in two basic styles: envelope, or flat; and box style, or those with side gussets. Side gussets, some up to nine inches deep, give the pack a box shape and allow more volume. But they also cause packs to pull down and backwards because gravity always tends to make the items in the pack sink, giving the pack a slightly pregnant shape. This increases the distance from the back of the pack to the middle of your own center of gravity. The deeper the pack, the more you must lean forward to offset that pull.

Envelope packs, like the original #3 Duluth Pack, form a shape, when tightly filled, of a common sofa throw pillow, tapered to each edge. Since the deepest part of an envelope-style pack can only be in its exact middle, these packs keep weight higher in the pack and nearer your center of gravity.

Fabric for packs
- ❏ Nylon resists abrasion
- ❏ Cotton canvas gives and stretches
- ❏ PVC nylon is waterproof

Keep shoulder straps tight so the pack rides high and snug on your back

Envelope packs also fit the contour of canoes best and can slide under thwarts and the like, making the most efficient use of space.

Most people who complain about such traditional packs being uncomfortable probably have suffered with one that was improperly loaded and had its shoulder straps adjusted too loosely. With any pack that does not have a hip belt, shoulder straps must be kept tight. They should be no looser than necessary: you should just be able to squeeze into the shoulder straps. If the straps are loose, the pack pulls down and back, causing strain. Loose straps on a box-style pack are even more painful.

While envelope-style packs work best for gear, a box-style pack is more convenient as a food pack. Some folks put a cardboard box in their food pack to give rigidity and to protect the food, and this works well, though the box is relatively short lived. Others use a plastic garbage can. A few new packs use foam liners for protection and rigidity. Although I haven't used one of these, I suspect they would perform well.

Cruiser Combo

By far the best food pack I've ever used is the Cruiser Combo made by Duluth Tent and Awning. Using a technique that has been around for a long time, this pack contains a rugged ash pack basket inside the famous #2 Cruiser pack with added side pockets. This combination provides enough storage for the food needs of two for a week-long trip, as well as being extremely rugged protection for that food. A #3 Cruiser Combo is available for those with larger appetites.

We place a heavy six-mil plastic liner bag between the basket and the pack for water resistance, although many of the foods will be additionally waterproofed in plastic bags as well. The interior plastic wrappings also contain spills and food odors (to keep the bears from locating it). Each morning we transfer the luncheon items to one side pocket and in the other we keep a water bottle, knife, gorp, and other frequently needed items. Because of this, it is rarely necessary to dig around in the pack when we take lunch break or retrieve a quick-energy snack.

On long trips it is easier to use two small food packs than one large one. Food is very heavy, and large packs filled to the brim are a painful burden on portages and difficult to properly hang to put them out of reach of bears. Small packs fit in the canoe better and allow you to keep the canoe trimmed more easily.

If you are traveling with children, include small packs for them. Kids can use their school book bags or your old daypacks. Stuff their sleeping bags, raincoats, or other light items into their packs. Not only will it give them a real sense of being part of the adventure, but it helps to eliminate some of the bulk that would otherwise need to go in the canoe packs. It also gives them a place to store their special secret goodies they pick up along the way: colored rocks, pine cones, and other magic things.

Day pack

Sleeping Bags

To sleep well on a canoe trip is to enjoy your canoe trip. And sleeping well requires a good sleeping bag.

Most people enter the canoe country with far too much sleeping bag. Other than spring and fall camping, it will be a rare summer night that will see the temperature fall below forty degrees. Still, most people use a three-season bag, one that is rated to twenty degrees.

Such bags have two disadvantages. First, they can be uncomfortably warm. If they have a two-way zipper, opening the bottom for a foot or so will help create a draft that will make sleeping comfortable. But even if you do this, you still end up lugging around a bag much heavier and larger than is needed.

Sleep well, waken rested, and you'll enjoy your canoe trip

27

Summer bags, rated to thirty or forty degrees, are best suited to the canoe country. They will stuff to a smaller size for packing than their warmer counterparts and still provide adequate insulation. Remember that by sleeping in a tent and on some type of foam pad you'll add ten degrees to any bag's comfort rating, so the lighter bags serve quite well. Should the temperature drop to an unexpected low, you can add warmth by wearing some clothing.

The subject of the type of fill generates a lot of debate but really concerns only two basic types: synthetics and down. Most quality synthetics are so similar to each other as to be indistinguishable in use, no matter what the manufacturers' advertising hype. Down gets measured on its fill power (or how many cubic inches an ounce will fill). It makes no matter if the down comes from ducks or geese as long as it has a rating of about 550 fill power. Just make sure the down product you purchase says "down," not "down and feathers". Feathers, with their hard quills, poke through the bag and leak out. They also break down more quickly, shortening the life span of the bag.

Synthetics meet a real need, but this need is more in the realm of price than performance. Much is made of a synthetic bag's ability to keep you warm when it is wet, and this claim is true. But even if you capsize, there is little chance of ever getting your bag wet if your pack is properly waterproofed and you purchase a quality tent, so the value of this benefit is greatly exaggerated. The biggest advantage to a polyester-fill bag is that it will cost about one-half to two-thirds what a similar down model costs.

And that, I believe, is the extent of their advantages. The disadvantages outweigh them. Synthetic fills have a much shorter lifespan. They are made from precious, polluting petroleum. And they take a great amount of space in your pack. Despite all the claims, I've yet to find a synthetic bag that even comes close to down for compressibility.

Synthetics fills

- ❏ Are bulky
- ❏ Deteriorate more rapidly
- ❏ Are made from petroleum
- ❏ Are relatively inexpensive
- ❏ Are warm even when wet

Down fill

- ❏ Is warm for its weight
- ❏ Compresses well
- ❏ Has a long useful life
- ❏ Is useless when wet
- ❏ Is relatively expensive

Down bags do cost more and are susceptible to wetting. But in twenty-five years of canoe travel I have never soaked my bag. The greater cost is offset by the fact that a down bag, well cared for, may be the last bag you'll ever purchase.

I switched to synthetics once. After four years the fill in the bag (which was one of the industry leaders) wore out, turning to loose low-loft lumps. I returned to an aged down bag that was already fifteen years old, and I continued to use that bag until the nylon shell (not the down) wore out.

The one exception regarding synthetic fill bags would be for children. First, you'll not likely find a down bag for kids. Second, even if you could, you probably wouldn't want to shell out the kind of money it would take for something they'll outgrow. Finally, if anyone can get a sleeping bag wet or dirty, it's a kid. Fortunately, some very nice children's bags are offered in synthetic fills at pretty reasonable prices. Buy a good bag for your little camper. It will pay big dividends in comfort and happiness. The surest way to guarantee a newcomer to camping will never again want to go is to let him or her get cold, wet, or hungry. If having someone special enjoy the canoe country is important to you, make sure the person has good gear. This is true for adults as well as children.

Quality synthetic fill bags for children
- ❏ Readily available
- ❏ Washable
- ❏ Inexpensive

For me, the biggest advantage to down is its compressibility. Our two summer-weight down bags, in a compression stuff sack, are about the size of a single loaf of Wonder Bread. Obviously, no matter how you pack, this savings in space is wonderful, but especially so if you are striving to single portage by getting the gear of two people into one pack. Two synthetic bags of the same weight would take up at least three times the space of our two bags.

Even if (or maybe especially if) you do stick with a synthetic-fill bag, a compression stuff sack is a good idea. Two types of compression stuff sacks are available: one makes your bag a long cylinder; the other squashes it into a ball shape. Both work by means of straps that, once the bag is stuffed into the sack, are gradually tightened, compressing the bag to its minimum size. Of the two types, the cylinder compression stuff sack provides you with an end shape that best fits the confines of a Duluth Pack.

Most moderate- to high-quality sleeping bags are built in the semi-mummy shape, which is slightly tapered. This style is by far the most efficient since it reduces weight; but, more importantly, it decreases the amount of dead air that surrounds your body, allowing you to heat the bag more efficiently. Some folks complain that the bags are restrictive, and some models are; but there are enough tapered bags on the market that offer a good compromise between room and shape that, with a little shopping around, the buyer should find one that is suitable.

Sleeping pads

This is a simple subject. If you can afford one, buy a Therm-a-Rest pad. I hesitate to describe particular products in a book, because a book has a long life, and products come and go. But the Therm-a-Rest pad is so marvelous, I can hardly believe it won't be available for years to come. A wonderful idea, this pad is open-cell foam surrounded by an airtight nylon skin. Open the valve and the pad inflates. Want it harder? Blow it up like an air mattress. It is comfortable and durable and it rolls up to a very small package.

Most folks opt for a pad that is "three-quarter" length, about four feet long. It saves weight and space and your clothing can be put under the foot end of your bag to provide insulation there.

Other than comfort, insulation is the major reason to use a pad. When you crawl into your sleeping bag the fill beneath your body is compressed to virtually nothing, allowing rapid transfer of heat away from you and into the ground. A pad eliminates this, as well as the stiffness that comes from sleeping directly on the ground.

Sleeping pads

- ❏ Closed cell—warm, but not too comfortable
- ❏ Open cell—comfortable, but absorbs moisture
- ❏ Air mattress—comfortable but not too durable
- ❏ Open cell in airtight skin—warm, lightweight, comfortable, durable

Other acceptable pads are closed-cell types or open-cell encased in nylon. Because the Therm-a-Rest pad is airtight, it is also watertight. But most open-cell pads are literally sponges, so be careful. Closed-cell materials, such as ensolite, can't absorb water and are excellent insulators. They aren't nearly as comfortable, however, as open-cell pads.

A few diehards still use air mattresses, and certainly some of the very light backpacking models are wonders for size and weight. But durability is always a problem. For rough use, stick with a foam pad.

Miscellaneous gear

Stoves and cooking gear we'll talk about in another chapter. Beyond your major gear purchases just discussed, there isn't too much else you'll need.

One item most would consider a necessity is a tarp, or rain fly. Choose a good urethane nylon model, at least ten feet by twelve. Strung up near the cooking area on a drizzly day, a rain fly can turn a dismal experience into a fun one. I keep a ten- or twelve-foot chunk of parachute cord tied permanently to each grommet on the tarp so that the whole thing can be pitched in minutes. Just weave each piece back and forth, in a series of S-curves, until within inches of the tarp and then bind them with the loose end in the middle with a half hitch. They'll stay tangle-free until needed.

Axes and saws are matters of great debate, but your rule here should be simple. On short trips, less than a week in length, an ax is hardly worth the weight. Carrying fuel for your camp stove will be easier and lighter and will allow you to cook even on days when dry wood is hard to find. In most instances you'll be able to gather enough dry wood without needing an ax to split it. Using a folding saw, or just leaning the pieces against a log and stomping on them, will reduce wood to usable lengths. For cooking, small-diameter pieces are best anyway.

I often add an ax on long trips where fuel weight begins to equal ax weight, or in early spring or late fall when a fire could be a lifesaver if needed after a frigid swamping. We prefer to cook on wood most of the time, and we invariably want dry wood in wet conditions. Hence the ax. But this is really only a nod toward romanticism, for an amount of fuel equaling the weight of an ax would probably last a month with modern stoves.

Should you purchase an ax, a cruising ax of about two pounds is ideal. Stay away from hatchets. They are a hazard because their short length means a misplaced blow will likely swing right into the chopper's knee. An ax, with its long handle, will usually bury itself in the ground or chopping block before reaching your leg. Keep the ax extremely sharp and you'll not have to wind up and swing like a falling drawbridge to split wood. A sharp ax is both safer and easier to use than a dull one.

A number of folding saws on the market all seem to work well. I like the Sven Saw. Even a saw with a short blade of ten inches will cut all the wood you're likely to need.

Some guide books recommend bringing a stone and file for sharpening axes, saws, and knives on canoe trips. Nonsense. If your ax and saw won't stay sharp for a week, throw them away. On all but very long trips, sharpening before you leave is more than adequate. The only exception is your fillet knife, which should be sharpened about every other fish. I bring a very tiny ceramic sharpener for this task.

You'll want some rope and parachute cord. About fifty feet of each should do, unless your group has two food packs. In this case plan on a length of cord and rope per food pack. The rope should be nylon and at least one-quarter inch in diameter. The rope, and sometimes the parachute cord, are used in hanging your food pack. The rope is for hoisting and hanging the pack; the parachute cord is sometimes used to swing the hanging pack further away from the

Folding saw

tree to get the pack out of the reach of bears. We'll talk about these techniques later in the book. You may be tempted to use only parachute cord for hanging packs because it is strong enough. Don't do it. The thin-diameter cord stretches and is terribly hard on your hands as you pull on it while hoisting the pack.

Parachute cord is handy for making clotheslines and stringing up tarps. I usually stuff a few short lengths of cord in my pants pocket as well. You'll find these pieces useful for a thousand odd jobs.

Each person should carry a pocket knife, compass, and waterproof match safe at all times. A two-ounce bottle of bug dope usually finds its way into our pockets as well. Other than your personal toiletries, a few toys such as cameras and fishing tackle, and necessities such as a first aid kit and cooking equipment, the above-mentioned gear pretty much covers the gamut.

Equipment is a means to an end

Equipment helps to bridge the gap between skill and comfort. Obviously, the Ojibwa who left camp on a hunting trip with only his weapon, flint and tinder, and knife would laugh at us with all of our gadgets. But we lack his skill to make things from forest products as we need them. And even if we could do just that, with the number of people visiting the wilderness these days, the forest would suffer abuse. Balance your needs and decide whether the piece of equipment you want to include is essential, or essentially a waste. Consider carefully when purchasing camping gear. In some instances your health and safety may depend upon your choices. If you choose these major pieces of equipment carefully and purchase for quality and simplicity, most of these products will last for a lifetime of canoe camping.

And you won't end up wet and shivering like that sad couple in the discount-store tent.

Miscellaneous gear list
- ❏ Urethane rain fly
- ❏ Folding saw or ax
- ❏ Rope
- ❏ Parachute cord
- ❏ Pocket knife
- ❏ Compass
- ❏ Waterproof match safe
- ❏ Bug dope
- ❏ First aid kit
- ❏ Cameras
- ❏ Fishing tackle

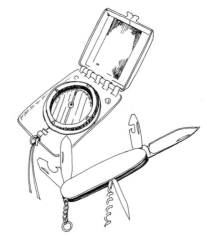

Compass and knife

Canoes and Paddles
for the Wilderness

We sat forlornly windbound as we watched the waves, and also the remainder of our outing, blow by. Frankly, I was a bit annoyed; not at the wind, which follows its own will and wasn't consciously disrupting our trip. I was annoyed at the choice of canoe that the other half of our foursome had made for this wilderness trip.

I looked at it as it sat on the beach. A super-lightweight, straight-keeled, low-bowed, shallow rocket of a boat, it was absolutely out of place in the wilderness. Because of its design, we sat an entire day watching the waves, knowing it would be foolhardy to venture abroad in a canoe that would turn into a submarine. The irony was that the rolling seas were not beyond the paddling skills of our party—just beyond the design of the canoe. The other boat, the one Mary Jo and I were paddling in those days, could easily handle the waves. The fellow who brought the rocket-canoe said to me, when I grumpily complained at sitting and watching waves, that his canoe was much faster than mine and that is why he selected it.

Now I ask you, how fast is a canoe that can't be put safely into the water? Granted, our canoe was a bit slower than theirs, but we could have easily paddled twenty miles that day while they sat idle. Now whose is faster? During the week as we traveled together, though our boat carried more

The wrong canoe can become a submarine

weight (theirs hadn't enough freeboard to carry the food pack), we rarely were more than a minute or two behind them as we reached portages, even when the paddling distance had been nearly ten miles.

So how fast is fast? A very debatable question. Far more important in a wilderness canoe is versatility. The ideal wilderness canoe is a joy to paddle, is maneuverable, has ample cargo capacity, and can handle other than perfect paddling conditions. Unfortunately, many people purchase canoes based on speed and weight—important criteria, yes, but not more so than the others.

That's not to say that whatever canoe you own, or can borrow, won't work on your canoe trip. Canoes don't have a brain, but you do. You can compensate for most deficiencies in your boat by altering plans, techniques, or timing. Don't ever let equipment (unless it is unsafe) prevent you from spending time afield. Skills are more important than goodies, so work to develop them.

However, should you be considering the purchase of a canoe, you need to determine which are the most important aspects of design for your needs. If your canoe will be used primarily for wilderness paddling, your choice will be very different than if your primary interest were in canoe racing. If you hunt or fish a lot out of a canoe, those factors must be considered. If you have physical limitations regarding the amount of weight you can lift, this becomes an additional criterion.

First, some generalities about canoes. Long canoes are faster than short ones. Beamy (wide) canoes are slower, but more stable, than narrow models. Deep canoes handle larger loads than shallow models. Flat-bottom canoes are more stable than round or V-shaped hulls, but are slower paddling. Straight-keeled canoes track a straight line better than canoes with a lot of rocker (end-to-end banana-shaped curve in the hull). Rockered canoes turn more quickly.

Now keep in mind that those are generalities. The ideal

What are your needs?

❑ Wilderness paddling

❑ Canoe racing

❑ Hunting

❑ Fishing

❑ Long portages

❑ White water

choice for the inexperienced or for those who travel with children. Loaded with gear, they become appreciably more steady, but once unloaded they'll feel like a pony that wants to roll in the grass. If you do much fishing, you'll probably not like a round-bottom boat.

In the middle are canoes that have slightly rounded or shallow V-shaped hulls. These are an excellent compromise in speed and stability and are very versatile. They handle rough water better than a flat-bottom hull, and are shallower drafting than the round-bottom models. Similarly, they are faster than the former, but slower than the latter.

Now step to the side of the overturned canoe and examine the keel line. Don't confuse the term *keel line* with the actual keel. A keel is a real protrusion of material, an inch or so tall and very narrow, down the length of the hull; it ostensibly improves tracking but is largely unnecessary. On aluminum canoes it merely functions to hold the two halves together. A well-designed canoe is a keel. *Keel line* merely refers to the bottom of the canoe in a straight line from the bow to stern. Many modern canoes are straight from end to end. They track (go straight) well and are fast. They are a nightmare to turn since the straight hull resists movement to the side.

The opposite extreme is a canoe with a great deal of end-to-end curve, which is called rocker. This kind of canoe turns very quickly and is the choice for whitewater paddlers; it works reasonably well for flat-water tripping when it is fully loaded. Unloaded, however, such a canoe will handle poorly in the wind since the bow and stern will rise above the water, in effect allowing the canoe to spin on its axis. Moderate rocker is the norm on good versatile wilderness tripping canoes. I would always opt for a canoe with some rocker over a straight model because of this versatility. The little bit of speed lost is compensated by the ease with which the canoe can be drawn sideways into landings, and ferried

Keel line influences tracking

❏ Straight line—fast, tracks well

❏ Moderate rocker—a good balance of speed, tracking, and maneuverability

❏ Extreme rocker—slower, turns readily

(moved sideways while moving forward) across rapids or windy bays and by the sheer fun of paddling such hulls.

Bow height is often discussed but is really a misunderstood factor. Straight-hulled boats commonly come with very low bow and stern profiles. The angle from the keel line to the tip of bow or stern is often very nearly ninety degrees. This does make the canoe faster since it increases the effective length of the canoe (more of it is in the water since it doesn't begin to curve upward a foot or two back from the bow). Usually manufacturers also claim such a design offers less resistance to a crossing wind. In the wilderness, however, these designs show their flaws. Unless severely flared out a few feet back from the bow (which decreases the speed advantage), they cut through, rather than ride up, a wave. Remember the story of our windbound experience? Water will quickly spill into the canoe as it knifes through a big wave, which is both annoying and dangerous. In shallow water these hulls are a pain because the bow strikes underwater obstructions that a more traditionally designed upswept bow would miss or slide past. Ever notice how many of these canoes you see with duct tape on the bows? A few hard whacks at full paddling speed can easily cause leaks.

Traditional canoes, and many modern compromise hulls, avoid these problems by incorporating a rising bow. Not only does the rising bow eliminate the problems of the low bow, it adds to the maneuverability of the canoe and, to my eye, is far more aesthetically pleasing. The degree of curve is proportionate to the degree to which it eliminates the aforementioned problems. However, most people will be happy with a moderately rising bow.

What about the crosswind argument? This is a highly overrated claim. Since you'll likely not even be able to get out onto the water with the straight, low-bowed canoe if the wind is bad enough to be a real factor, what possible difference can it make? Our old wood and canvas Chestnut-style

Bow profile affects safety

- ❑ Flat and low—faster, waves spill in
- ❑ Traditional upswept—rides up safely on waves, not available in mass-produced canoes
- ❑ Moderate rising—rides safely in high seas, available

Cruiser, built by Stewart River Boatworks in Two Harbors, Minnesota, has very traditional, very high-profile bow and stern. It handles big seas better than any canoe I've ever seen or paddled and is a real comfort in such situations. I can't remember ever shipping a drop of water over the bow, even in three-foot waves. At the same time, owing to other well-designed hull features, it is extremely fast and maneuverable and has never been difficult to handle in a crosswind.

Think about this for a moment. Light crosswinds aren't going to blow a well-designed canoe sideways, no matter what the profile of the bow and stern. And in a heavy wind, only a lunatic would paddle at ninety degrees to the wind. Instead, you paddle directly into, or slightly quartering, the wind and waves. The higher profile isn't presented to the wind since it is now knifing into it. But a rising bow does add a tremendous safety factor in assuring you don't nosedive to the bottom of the lake. When the winds are bad, I'd prefer an upswept, rising bow every time.

You'll probably notice that the majority of modern canoes do not have the more traditional designs, the graceful curve to the bow and stern. The amount of curve to the bow is actually quite irrelevant unless it is exaggerated to the point that it begins to use up valuable cargo capacity. Modern canoes have no curve because they are created on a form and it would be impossible to remove them from that form if the bow and stern curved back upon themselves. Another factor is that these canoes are shipped to dealers without the seats and thwarts installed, allowing them to nest together like a cook kit and thereby saving considerable shipping expense. In other words, although the majority of canoes you'll look at have nearly vertical bow and stern, this is not so much a matter of good design as it is convenience for the manufacturer.

Most good wilderness tripping canoes are about thirteen inches deep amidships, which is an excellent compromise.

Hull depth affects load capacity and wind resistance

❏ 12 inches—small load capacity, light

❏ 13 inches—a good balance of load capacity, weight, and handling ease

❏ 15 inches—large load capacity, hard to handle in crosswinds

You can get by with only twelve inches, and some expedition models have as much as fifteen. Depth amidships will affect paddling ease and load capacity. The deeper the hull, the greater the load capacity. Unloaded, a fifteen-inch-deep canoe can be a real bear to handle in a crosswind. I know, I just disputed the importance of bow height in such situations. However, adding two inches of height to the profile of a canoe down its entire length does begin to seriously raise the susceptibility to wind, but only when the canoe is unloaded. If you paddle on extended journeys to the Arctic, a fifteen-inch-deep hull will probably be necessary. If you stick to the flatwater wilderness of Minnesota and Ontario, thirteen inches will do admirably and can still handle more arduous tasks should the situation arise.

What we end up with, then, is a canoe about seventeen feet long, thirteen inches deep, with a moderate amount of rocker, slightly upswept ends, and either a shallow V or somewhat rounded bottom. A canoe as just described will turn quickly when needed, track well when it must, handle a load safely in all types of seas, and maintain good flatwater paddling speed. Fortunately, there are many models available that meet these requirements. Many canoe shops have demonstration days or provide for rental, so the prospective buyer can paddle canoes before purchasing. This is a wise thing to do: make sure you test paddle the canoe both fully loaded and empty and, if feasible, in both rough water and calm. If the weather and water are warm, you might also consider trying to tip test canoes over in shallow water (wear your personal flotation device). Every canoe owner should know at just what point his or her canoe will capsize. You might also inquire of outfitters which models they rent. If you can find a rental canoe of the sort you wish to buy, using it on an actual canoe trip would be the best test of all.

Such a canoe will probably be available in a few different hull materials. Common materials are wood, fiberglass,

Kevlar, and plastic. Aluminum is used in many canoes, but not often in the hull design just described. Generally, aluminum canoes are flat-bottom canoes built for stability and used primarily by those interested in fishing or hunting. It is a good choice for a hull material, being very durable and reasonably light, but so far hasn't been adopted into high-performance designs. It also has its drawbacks, which include being very noisy, cold to the touch, and prone to leakage when rivets become loose and having a tendency to grab ahold of any rock it contacts.

Plastic hulls, such as Royalex and polyethylene, are fast replacing the aluminum models as work-horse canoes. They are probably the most durable of hulls, are very quiet, slip easily over rocks, and come in hull designs suitable for wilderness work, and some are fairly light in weight. There are also some real clunkers out there. Stay away from plastic hulls that use structural stiffeners of aluminum tubing or similar ridiculous additions. Aluminum and plastic bend at different rates, and recover unequally, leaving you with a canoe that will never again have a flat bottom should you be unfortunate enough to take a blow in whitewater or get high-centered on some lurking canoe-eating boulder midlake.

Of the two plastic materials, Royalex still is the better choice, though it is more expensive. Because it is a laminate, Royalex can be beefed up in areas of high impact or where stiffness is needed. A polyethylene canoe of equal durability and stiffness will always be heavier because it is a solid material, which means that in order to be thicker in the bow, it must retain that thickness throughout the hull. A Royalex canoe, thick and stiff only where needed, will be ten to twenty percent lighter than a polyethylene canoe with identical hull shape. Plastic canoes do have a tendency to "oil can," which means they flex along the floor when passing over waves. This can be a little disconcerting to some folks, and probably reduces the paddling efficiency a bit, but is not a serious drawback. It is just the nature of the beast.

A versatile wilderness canoe

- ❏ Seventeen feet long
- ❏ Thirteen inches deep
- ❏ Moderate rocker
- ❏ Slightly upswept ends
- ❏ Shallow V hull
- ❏ Plastic or fiberglass

Watch out for factory seconds in either of these materials. Since both types are molded, factory seconds are often much heavier than they're supposed to be because someone slipped up and pumped a little too much goo into the mold. They're fine for the cabin, but a burden on a portage.

Plastic hulls are just about the perfect compromise for many canoeists, especially if you're a little hard on equipment. Polyethylene hulls are priced near aluminum; Royalex is near the price of fiberglass, which is about half the price of Kevlar. A couple of excellent hull designs are now available in Royalex that weigh in at a surprisingly light sixty to sixty-five pounds.

Many excellent hulls are offered in fiberglass and Kevlar. Since these two materials are actually fabrics that are laid up on forms, they lend themselves well to fine entry lines and sophisticated hull shapes. Some of the best, and some of the worst, canoes for wilderness travel are made from fiberglass or Kevlar. Often identical models are available in both materials, with the major difference being weight and price. Fiberglass canoes usually weigh in around sixty to sixty-five pounds while their Kevlar counterparts will shed another ten pounds. Kevlar boats can run up to two thousand dollars. Those on a budget won't get any less canoe by purchasing a fiberglass model, only a bit more weight, and possibly some added durability. Kevlar's added strength allows the manufacturer to build lighter model canoes than are possible in fiberglass.

Some manufacturers carry this lightness thing too far, however, building fragile craft. For wilderness travel it would be a mistake to trade durability for light weight. Many buyers are very disappointed to find out when their canoe begins to leak that Kevlar isn't as bulletproof as they'd been led to believe.

Superlight models must be treated with great care because it is entirely possible to gouge, even puncture, these canoes. Some gouges are deep enough to cause leakage or to begin to create delaminations when water enters the weave. And unless you enjoy working with toxic chemicals, repairing such canoes is often neither simple or enjoyable.

I've seen some Kevlar boats reduced to leaky, epoxy-patched, ugly hulks in just a couple of years. Touching up scratches in the gel coat isn't the simplest thing, either. The best prevention is to beach your boat parallel to shore and wet-foot it, minimizing any chance for abrasion.

Some folks put a Kevlar skid plate on the bow to provide for extra protection. Skid plates do add durability, but they also increase the width of the canoe at the entry point, look ugly on a fine canoe, and would be largely unnecessary if the canoe wasn't rammed bow first up onto shore. Despite the current enthusiasm for Kevlar, the vast majority of leaking canoes I've seen in the last decade have all been made of this material, mostly because the owners believed the "bullet-proof" hype and failed to exercise the care these canoes really need. Because both Kevlar and fiberglass canoes are so susceptible to abrasion, it would be wise for you to treat them as carefully as you would a wood and canvas canoe.

A wood and canvas canoe should be a viable option, especially if you appreciate its great beauty, aren't afraid of a little upkeep, and realize that it is made of natural, biodegradable materials and was created with skillful hands. The cost is comparable to a fine Kevlar canoe. I wish everyone had the opportunity to paddle a fine wood and canvas canoe. No, we're not talking about a cedar strip canoe "like Uncle Bob built" in his garage. Strip canoes, though made of wood, are more akin to a fiberglass canoe, since they are covered, inside and out, with that material. The wood is laminated in the middle, largely to add substance and form, and could just as easily be strips of plastic or foam.

The wood and canvas canoe is really an adaptation of the Native American birch-bark canoe. Bark canoes were built

Canoe hull materials

❑ Aluminum

❑ Plastic laminate

❑ Fiberglass

❑ Kevlar

❑ Wood and canvas

by forming a hull of bark first, and then forcing the planking and ribs into the hull. The wood and canvas canoe was the white man's adaptation, in which the ribs were bent over a form, over which the planking was laid. The canvas served the purpose of the birch-bark: a waterproof outside cover. The real strength of a wooden canoe is the wood itself, which is almost always white or red cedar. That is why there is little advantage, and some disadvantages, in covering the wood with fiberglass instead of canvas (fiberglass is heavier than canvas, doesn't flex as readily and makes any canoe repair more difficult).

Since wood can be shaped in almost any fashion, excellent hull designs can be created. Built by a careful craftsman, a wood and canvas canoe can be very light (our seventeen-footer weighs sixty-three pounds, our sixteen-footer only fifty-five pounds). After using wood and canvas canoes on canoe trips up to thirty days in length and on countless other trips, I feel confident in asserting that they are at least as durable as the majority of fiberglass and Kevlar canoes given similar care or abuse.

They do require some maintenance, but not as much as you'd think, especially if stored indoors when not in use. Because upkeep means using such relatively pleasant things as a little paint or spar varnish, no special skills or serious toxins are involved. Properly maintained, wood and canvas canoes will not add much weight through water gain, despite all the stories you've heard. When we spent three months working for the Forest Service we used our own seventeen-foot wood and canvas canoe. After a summer of hard use and exposure, the canoe weighed three pounds more at the end of August than it had at the first of June. Big deal.

The only accessories you'll need for your canoe are painter rings and a portage yoke. Painter rings are bow- and stern-mounted brass rings used for the attachment of ropes, either for towing a canoe or for lining a canoe upstream.

They are also invaluable for lash points when car-topping the canoe. Painter rings should be located low on the ends, very near the water line. Unfortunately, many modern canoes use the bow and stern as hollow floatation chambers, which is great for safety but makes drilling holes for, and attaching, painter rings unwise, if not impossible. These canoes generally have a hole on the top of the deck for attaching lines, which is barely adequate but about the only place left to attach a rope.

Be careful if you attach a rope to the deck top when towing or lining. Tied to the deck, the rope wants to pull the bow downward, which could cause the canoe to take a nosedive. Similarly, if the rope is off-centered because of the angle of the pull, the bow acts as a keel and wants to force the canoe quickly to one side.

A portage yoke is a must. No matter how light your canoe, portaging will be much more pleasurable with a well-fitted, padded yoke. The best yokes are adjustable for shoulder width. Though I've tried many kinds of yokes, from radically contoured to handcarved, I keep returning to a simple curved yoke fitted with adjustable, densely packed foam pads. If your canoe comes with a curved center thwart, you only need to purchase the pads. If it comes only with a straight thwart, remove it and bolt in its place an entire yoke assembly. Ash wood is about the best material for yokes since it has just enough spring to ease the bumps but won't easily break.

A great many new canoes come with "tractor seats," those butt-hugging contoured seats reminiscent of those on an old John Deere tractor. I hate them. They do not allow you to comfortably sit off center (which may be necessary to temporarily offset an imbalanced load), nor can you sit reversed in one, as you might if you were paddling a tandem canoe solo by using the bow as the stern. Often seats of this type are on rails, at least in the bow, to allow you to trim the

A portage yoke is essential
❑ Curved
❑ Adjustable
❑ Padded

Portage yoke

canoe for proper front-to-back weight balance. This is a nice feature if two paddlers of widely disparate weights are in an unloaded canoe, but is largely unnecessary on a wilderness trip, where trim is altered by shifting the cargo.

If you too don't like these seats, replace them with ash-framed cane seats. Cane seats soon take on your contours, keeping you from sliding around. They also breathe through the mesh, which is wonderful on both wet days and hot ones. And you can more easily trim side-to-side balance by sliding a bit to one side.

While some folks carry bailers (either a large sponge or a plastic bleach bottle with the large end cut off) to remove excess water from inside the canoe, you'll not find much need for these in the BWCAW or Quetico unless you do an awful lot of whitewater work. Even in a heavy rain, you'll not likely gather enough water in your canoe to make much difference between portages, where it is emptied when you pick up the canoe.

Canoe repair varies greatly depending upon the hull material, and it would be wise to contact the manufacturer to get advice. Most of us will need only to make temporary patch jobs while in the wilderness, and even these will likely be very rare. A small roll of duct tape is about all one will ever need to make temporary patches for holes in any canoe, no matter the hull material. Dry the canoe thoroughly before applying the tape.

While we've carried duct tape for years without having any need to use it, we have had need for an extra nut and washer a couple of times. It is wise to check the nuts on the bolts that hold your seat and thwarts in place before each canoe trip to make sure they are tight. One extra nut stashed in your gear is a nice precaution, because even if you make sure your canoe won't fall apart, you may find, as we have, that others aren't so careful. And you can charge an exorbitant price for a nut in the wilderness when your buddy's yoke suddenly falls off!

Canoe repair kit is simple but essential

❑ Duct tape

❑ Nuts, washers, and bolts

Select the right paddle

Of course a canoe can't do a doggone thing without someone wielding a paddle, and paddle choice is highly subjective. Like a wilderness canoe, a paddle for the bush country should be both versatile and durable.

You should purchase a paddle that weighs about twenty to twenty-five ounces, with a blade about eight inches in width. Straight-shaft paddles get the nod over bent shafts because of their versatility. It is much more awkward to do draw strokes with a bent shaft, and such paddles totally eliminate the possibility of doing other useful strokes, such as the Canadian or Indian. Yes, bent-shaft paddles will give you greater straight-ahead speed, but speed isn't the most important factor in the wilderness. And you can't fillet a fish on the blade of a bent shaft paddle. I know some canoeists who carry a straight-shaft paddle as their spare and use it where called for, using the bent shaft for straight-ahead paddling on large lakes.

Speaking of spare paddles, there should always be at least one for your group. Paddles do break occasionally, and traveling without an extra one is like not having a spare tire for your car. Eventually you are going to get into trouble.

Paddle grips come in an array of shapes these days: traditional archlike; T-grips; footballs; and unidirectional. Buy whatever feels best to your hand, but I suggest you purchase a paddle that doesn't have a unidirectional grip. These grips, which curve forward, can be used comfortably only when the paddle faces in one direction. On a bent-shaft paddle, which can only be used facing one way, such a grip makes sense. But on a straight-shaft paddle, which is identical on both sides of the blade and shaft, a grip that can be used in only one position only limits the paddle's versatility. As you perfect your paddle strokes you'll find some techniques that require that the paddle be rotated. A one-way

Always take along at least one extra paddle

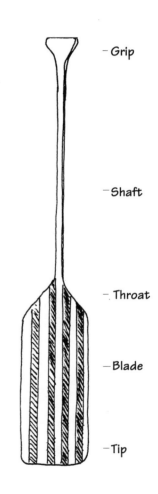

- Grip

- Shaft

- Throat

- Blade

- Tip

49

grip on an otherwise two-way paddle doesn't work well in these situations.

Blade shape varies from short and square to long and slender. Each type has advantages, but for a variety of tasks in the wilderness, an eight-inch-wide rectangular or oval blade is best. Most modern paddles are rectangular; of these, those with rounded tip corners splash less and are quieter than those with square tips. Oval blades actually are more similar to the shape of a beaver tail, which they are often called. These paddles are very quiet to use (which is important in wildlife photography or hunting) and don't splash when entering the water (makes a big difference in the spring and fall when the water is icy). The surface area of the blades will likely be about the same, and therefore, so is paddling efficiency. If you use short, rapid strokes, you'll likely find the shorter, wider blades easier to use.

The majority of paddles are made of laminated construction. Manufacturers can blend soft, light woods with stronger, more durable types to create a paddle with the best features of both. I suggest you look for a paddle that does not have a laminated shaft, however. A laminated shaft is very stiff, and a canoe paddle should have a very slight amount of spring in the shaft. Laminated blades are fine, though, and add durability. It is increasingly difficult for paddle builders to find clear, strong wood wide enough to make a one-piece paddle, but they are available, and a one piece paddle can be a real joy to use and a work of art.

Stick with wooden paddles. The plastic and aluminum kind that canoe liveries use are tough, but they are ugly and cold to the hand. The very expensive composite paddles are exceptionally light, but prone to breaking. Don't buy a cheap paddle, but don't think you need to buy the most expensive model either. In the middle range are a great number of fine paddles at moderate prices, paddles that will likely last you a lifetime if you don't use them as pry bars or push poles.

The most confusing aspect of buying a paddle is determining the correct length. What you are really concerned about is the length of the shaft from the grip to the top of the blade. With blades of all kinds of widths and lengths, the old routine of picking a paddle that comes up to your nose simply isn't accurate (if it ever was) because the blades affect overall paddle length. However, no matter the blade style, the key measurement for proper sizing is the length of the shaft, from the grip to the top of the blade. Once you find a shaft length comfortable for your style and canoe, you'll find it won't change more than an inch or two no matter the blade style.

The best way to choose the correct length is to sit in a chair with your legs slightly apart. Turn the paddle upside down so that the grip rests between your legs on the chair's seat. Your correct shaft length will be one that comes up to your nose, give or take a little. Racers may opt for a shorter paddle, wilderness trekkers a tad longer. Generally, from the chair to your nose, plus a hand's width (four to six inches) will give you the best length for wilderness use.

Selecting the proper canoe and paddles for your wilderness trips may seem a bit confusing at first, so take your time. This equipment will determine not only your pleasure afield but often your safety. And it should last a lifetime as well. Choose carefully. Give the nod toward durability and versatility over trendy designs or speed and lightness, and you should end up with equipment that will not only take you safely throughout the Boundary Waters and Quetico but become almost an extension of yourself.

A versatile wilderness paddle

❏ Made of wood

❏ Twenty to twenty-five ounces

❏ Straight, non-laminated shaft

❏ Two-way grip

❏ Eight inch wide, oval or rectangular, laminated blade

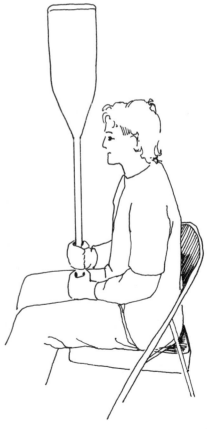

Canoe Country Clothing

You may not think it is important to make a fashion statement when on a canoe trip, but the fact is the clothing you choose for your adventure will indeed receive critical review. Wind and rain will test it, and insects will line up to assess your clothing choices. The sun will pass judgment and cold winds will pry into every flaw. The very rocks themselves will seek to make an impression. Satisfying all these critics takes a bit of forethought.

You'll also have a limited amount of space in your pack for clothing. Just what to cram into that space is a dilemma we each face when packing for a trip. We are all used to having an abundance of clothing at home to change into when new conditions arise or we are wet and dirty. Such luxury isn't an option on a canoe trip, not if you want your Duluth Packs to be smaller than a compact car. Mary Jo and I long ago gave up on carrying a complete change of clothing, finding, for the most part, that even on the longest of trips one set was enough, with the exception of a clean change of underwear and socks.

Sound too rugged? It really isn't. Most canoe trips to the BWCAW and Quetico are four- or five-day affairs. There is little chance you'll wear out quality clothes in that short a span of time. And a little dirt never hurt anyone. You're on a wilderness canoe trip, after all, not at the country club. If

Your clothing must stand up to harsh winds, cold rain, voracious insects, and abrasive rocks—and still be comfortable in the sunshine

Summer clothing checklist

Items to wear

❑ One pair loose-cut trousers (no blue jeans)

❑ One tight-weave, long-sleeve shirt (not blue)

❑ Cotton bandanna

❑ Hat

❑ T-shirt, underwear

❑ Wool socks

❑ Boots

Items to pack

❑ One long sleeve wool-type shirt

❑ One extra pair wool socks

❑ One change of T-shirt, underwear

❑ Rain jacket and pants

❑ Lightweight sneakers

❑ Athletic shorts/swimsuit

you're careful you won't end up with wet clothing. But what you do choose to wear and pack is of critical importance to both comfort and safety.

Canoe country clothing must be versatile and tough and do a number of important things: provide warmth, keep you dry, shield from insects and sunburn, be easy to care for, and be comfortable for paddling and portaging. Insulating garments should also have the ability to remain warm even if wet. During the spring or fall, additional items will likely be needed to keep you warm. The system we use is the layering system. Each garment works in coordination with the rest to supply you with both protection and comfort. For instance, your rain jacket does double duty as a windbreaker, and when combined with some type of insulating garment, provides more than adequate warmth for chilly days afield. Consider the checklists on this page and the next page.

As you can see, if you are wearing the specified items, there really isn't much left to pack. If you decide to do away with the sneakers and the swimsuit, you're left with just a change of underwear and socks. When you do pack your extra clothing, except the shoes, put them in a strong, small plastic bag or a nylon ditty bag. You'll be able to find things much easier this way and they will stay clean and dry. (A lot of good a wet, dirty change of clothes will do you!)

Since each clothing item you choose must serve a purpose, let's discuss each item in turn. Combined, this clothing will provide you with a layering system that will meet your demands in all canoeing weather.

Rain Gear

If you have a limited amount of money to spend on outdoor clothing, you could do no better than to spend most of it on rain gear. Invest in a good rain jacket and pants. Forget the ponchos. Invariably when it rains, it blows, making a poncho a much better sail than rain gear. A poncho also is dismal at protecting the lower body. Ditto for those cheap plastic rain suits. They're garbage—which is exactly where they end up after a few days afield.

A good rain jacket will have tight-fitting cuffs so water doesn't trickle in while you're paddling or when your arms are above your head while portaging a canoe. It should be about thigh-length and have a hood (preferably one that zips off). Rain pants should have zippers from hem to knee to allow for slipping them on over boots. A double layer of fabric on the seat and knees will make rain pants more durable and more waterproof (even the best waterproof fabrics can have moisture forced through them with the added pressure of sitting and kneeling). Make sure the zippers on both jacket and pants are covered by ample storm flaps. Underarm "pit zips" provide excellent ventilation when you're really exerting yourself but may occasionally allow in some rain water.

Remember, while waterproof fabric choice is important, all other things being equal, design is critical in determining how storm-proof a garment will be. For instance, pockets with inadequate storm flaps will catch water, soaking the inside of the jacket. Hoods that won't zip off collect moisture if not being worn and wick it right down the back of the jacket. Loose cuffs that allow water to reach your shirt will provide for even more wicking. A nice feature found on some lined rain jackets is a fabric "dam" of a nonabsorbent material around the inside of the hem. This prevents the inside lining from contacting water and then wicking it further into the jacket.

I prefer the new generation of waterproof, breathable fabrics, specifically Gore-Tex. I have used PVC and urethane-coated nylon rain gear and have found them stifling warm on rainy summer days, even those that are replete with protected vents that are supposed to allow for heat to escape. I don't know about you, but given the choice, I think I'd rather be wet with clean rain water than to soak my only set

Spring/fall clothing checklist

Items to wear

- ❏ One pair loose-cut, warm trousers (no blue jeans)
- ❏ One tight-weave, warm, long-sleeve shirt (not blue)
- ❏ Cotton bandanna
- ❏ Hat
- ❏ T-shirt, underwear
- ❏ Wool socks
- ❏ Boots

Items to pack

- ❏ One long sleeve wool-type shirt
- ❏ Jacket of polyester fleece or wool. Down is okay if kept dry
- ❏ Lightweight polypropylene or Thermax top (crew neck or zip turtleneck) and longjohns
- ❏ Light stocking cap of wool, Thermax or polypropylene
- ❏ Light wool or fleece gloves
- ❏ Rain jacket and pants
- ❏ One extra pair wool socks
- ❏ One change of T-shirt, underwear
- ❏ Lightweight sneakers

of clothing with perspiration and then have to live in those rather odoriferous garments for the better part of a week. However, nonbreathable fabrics, which are certainly very waterproof, are adequate in other respects and function well in cooler weather, when perspiration is less of a problem, or during sedentary activities such as fishing.

Gore-Tex has been around long enough now to be the industry standard. Although the early stuff had its problems, Gore has solved those (most were problems of design) by making every garment manufacturer pass rugged design and construction tests. And although other manufacturers have sought to knock Gore-Tex from the top of the heap, none of the other products that claim to be both waterproof and breathable really perform nearly as well as the original. Some we've tested actually perform worse than urethane-coated nylon or PVC rain wear. Others are very susceptible to dirt contamination and especially DEET, the most common insect repellent used. Others yet have a breathable-water-proof coating (Gore-Tex is a membrane) that wears off with washings and cracks in cold weather. Be wary.

The final criteria for rain gear are size and weight. All other things being nearly equal, the jacket and pants that weigh the least and stuff down to the smallest size are the ones you want in your pack. Since your rain gear will end up also being the outermost garment in your layering system, be sure that you purchase rain wear large enough to fit comfortably over other layers.

Shirt and pants

Is this guy going to tell us about such simple items as shirts and pants? Yes I am, and for good reason.

Sitting in a canoe for long periods of time wearing tight clothing is miserable. So is paddling wearing a restrictive shirt, and so is portaging, trying to throw that leg over a deadfall, with pants that are too tight. The worst offender in

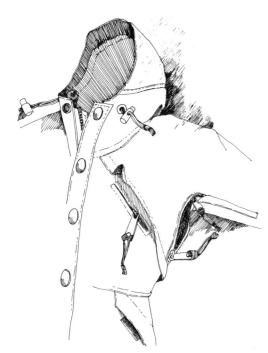

Well-designed rain jacket

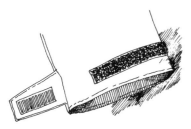

Adjustable cuffs

the pants department is the venerable blue jeans. Most styles, unless cut for laborers, are far too tight in all the wrong places. They may make your body look good, but they aren't made for real work. And that's what you'll be doing on a canoe trip. In addition, denim fabric soaks up water readily but is loath to let it go. Nothing seems to dry more slowly than do blue jeans. And when worn on warm days, dark jeans can become uncomfortably warm.

But why wear pants on hot days anyway? How about shorts? Well, that certainly is one way to go, and shorts can be a treat on hot days, provided you aren't susceptible to sunburn, you aren't portaging brushy trails, and the insects aren't biting. But when any of the above comes into play, which is frequently the case in the canoe country, long pants are a blessing.

Loose-fitting pants and long-sleeve shirts, woven of lightweight and light color material, are the best choice: not too warm for hot but buggy days, not so thick they won't dry readily, and not so restrictive as to cut off your blood flow. The most important function of shirts and pants is protection from bugs, brush, and sun. Therefore, make sure they are light and cool enough to wear on warm days when protection can be needed.

Save yourself some money and go to the work-clothing department of your favorite store. Clothing that was made for laborers is light, tough, cheap and cut for freedom of movement. Most pants and shirts are made of a cotton/polyester blend that wears well and dries readily. You could spend a lot of money for "camping clothes" complete with designer labels, but it is usually too pricey and generally is pretty wimpy.

Over the years I've noticed that blue clothing, from robin's egg to royal in hue, seems to attract black flies. If someone you don't like is going on a canoe trip, why don't you give him or her a nice blue shirt? Otherwise, stay away from blue clothing.

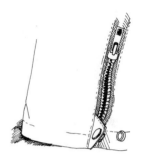

Long zippers on rain pants

Blue clothing tends to attract black flies

A broad-brimmed hat
is essential

Hats

Consider a hat a must. It keeps biting insects out of your hair, protects you from sun and rain, and shields your eyes from glare. I like hats with a wide brim around the perimeter of the hat. Fur felt is a better choice than wool felt because it shrinks less. Some nice canvas models are available as well. The advantages of such hats are that they extend protection to the back of your neck and the wide brim holds a mosquito head-net nicely away from your face. Such hats also make a great bellows for encouraging reluctant campfires.

During spring and fall, a light stocking cap can be a real blessing on chilly days; and when worn at night it will help you keep warmer while sleeping. Remember, you lose more body heat through your head than any one other spot on your body.

Boots

I was half tempted to devote a whole chapter to boots, since preferences are as varied as are the canoeists who wear them. But for all intents and purposes, your canoeing style will determine what type of boots to wear. Notice I said boots, not footwear. Anyone who humps over a rugged portage with a pack and canoe and isn't wearing boots that provide ankle support is an accident waiting to happen. Every sprained or broken ankle I've ever seen in the wilderness was a result of inadequate, unsupportive footwear (usually sneakers).

How does style dictate your boot choice? Well, canoeists can generally be divided into two different camps: wet-foot and dry-foot.

Dry-foot canoeists abuse their canoes and paddles by ramming their boat up on the rocks and pushing even farther with their paddles. They then let the canoe grind on the rocks as they struggle to get out (usually by walking up the center of the rocking canoe) just so they can get their dainty little tootsies to shore without getting wet. Then they drag their poor canoe up the boulder-strewn bank so they can get at their packs, making enough noise to disturb everyone within a five-mile radius.

These are also the same folks who, when encountering a wet, muddy spot on the portage, throw every kind of ankle-busting stump and branch into the mud, trying to build some kind of bridge upon which to walk. Or worse yet, they migrate to the outside of the mudhole, widening it and causing erosion.

As you can see, I don't much care for this method.

The other faction is the wet-foot canoeists. These folks position their canoe parallel to the shore, step out into the water, and then unload. The canoe is picked up, usually without it ever touching land.

On portages, since their feet are wet already, a little mud doesn't stop these people and they willingly tromp through wet spots. Wet-foot canoeists usually pass through without much commotion.

Surprisingly, these two distinct groups often wear the same footgear, the major difference being that the wet-footers don't mind getting wet. Most experienced paddlers I've seen choose to wear a six- or eight-inch tall unlined leather work boot. Leather stands up to repeated wettings and dryings much better than synthetics (really!) if treated regularly with some type of leather grease. A lot of synthetic boots, especially those euphemistically called "hiking boots," are really little better than hightop sneakers. Usually made of vinyl or nylon, or a combination, they really offer little ankle support. One brand we tested had, in the footbed, a midsole of a cardboard-type product, which deteriorated quickly under wet conditions.

Stay away from boots with deeply lugged hard rubber soles. Fine for dry mountain work, on wet rocks and logs such soles are treacherous, slipping readily. A lugged sole of softer rubber is fine, as are the moderately patterned soles of most work boots.

While we prefer the wet-foot method, I have to admit I don't relish wet feet, especially in spring or fall. We searched for a waterproof boot that was suited to our needs and found only one that worked well—the venerable rubber-bottom, leather-top L.L. Bean Maine Hunting Shoe.

You see, most waterproof leather boots are only eight inches tall, and most landings will require a bit more "free board" than that or water will rush over the top. We also found most were insulated as well, not something particularly desired for summer canoeing. But the Bean boot comes both uninsulated and in a multitude of heights. Since the tongue is fully gusseted (meaning it is sewn in the full height of the boot—be careful, many imitators are not) water doesn't rush in. Bean doesn't advertise this boot as fully waterproof, and indeed, as it comes from them, it isn't. The seam where the leather top is sewn to the rubber bottom leaks unless treated with Sno-Seal.

This concoction is a paste that we pack into the seams, heating the boot surface with a blow drier, until the stitching holes (and the entire leather uppers) are saturated. Sno-Seal is wonderful waterproofing and the only brand we've found that works well. Really saturate the boots when you first get them, packing Sno-Seal into every stitch and all over the leather, until, even after repeated heatings with the blow drier, the boot simply won't absorb any more paste. After that, usually, one good treatment prior to a trip will last the duration. On trips of a week or more, take some extra Sno-Seal for retreatment.

One important tip: the first time you step into cool water with hot feet in these boots, the capillary action caused by the temperature difference will suck water through even the most Sno-Seal–packed stitching. After this first episode, the leather swells around the stitching holes and leakage

Leather boot with rubber sole

ceases. To avoid this syndrome, try putting your boots on the day before you depart and stand in some water, such as in your bathtub, and let them absorb water. The inside will have enough time to dry overnight before you begin your trip, but the leather will still be swollen enough to keep water from entering.

The advantages of the Bean boot are weight (relatively light), excellent ankle support, and soft rubber sole for good traction. They are also resolable, for about one-third the cost of a new pair, if you send them back to L.L. Bean. I get about one year's wear before resoling, but then we are in the wilderness thirty to forty days a year and I also wear these boots for hunting.

Since it doesn't do any good to have a waterproof boot so short that water pours in over the top, order boots tall enough. We've used both twelve- and fourteen-inch boots and prefer the latter. By the way, Bean doesn't offer these heights in women's sizes, but often women can wear a small men's in the narrow width. We had them build custom-made fourteen-inchers for Mary Jo on a women's sole for a few extra bucks. Make sure you order the optional lacing hooks or you'll spend the whole morning lacing up your tall boots.

Some folks wear rubber knee boots, especially in the spring and fall when the water is really chilly. If you can find a pair that fit well without your heel slipping, they'll work quite well, although they don't provide the greatest ankle support. In the summer they are unbearably hot.

Whether you opt to keep your feet dry or get them wet, boots are the only sensible way to go. The wilderness is no place for a badly sprained ankle.

Sneakers

Yes, sneakers have their place in the canoe country. When you're walking your canoe up or down a shallow stream, they

An ideal boot for canoeists

- ❏ Good ankle support
- ❏ Fully gusseted tongue
- ❏ Leather
- ❏ Waterproofed
- ❏ Soft rubber sole
- ❏ 14 inches high
- ❏ Lacing hooks

are great. While you're lounging in camp, they give your feet comfort and protection while your boots air in the sun.

I read one book written by an ex-guide from the canoe country who insisted his clients leave their sneakers behind, maintaining that they weren't going to get their feet wet. Obviously, if you ram your boat up on shore, don't portage in the rain, stay away from muddy trails (HOW?), you might keep your feet dry. But I've never seen those conditions in Minnesota or Ontario. Even if you do manage to arrive in camp with dry feet, sneakers reduce campsite impact and compaction because of their soft soles, as well as allow you to air your boots in the sun of day, instead of only at night.

Just make sure you take the lightest pair you can find. Nylon jogging shoes are excellent because they offer good support, have soles designed with traction in mind, and are very light. Since you'll only be wearing them a few hours a day, there is no sense in hauling along any more weight than is necessary. Are sneakers a luxury? Maybe. But they are one luxury we afford ourselves.

Socks

Your choice of socks is at least as important as that of boots. Cotton or synthetic athletic socks are not a good choice. They won't keep your feet warm when wet, tend to bunch up under the balls of feet or heels (leading to blisters), and dry slowly.

A canoe country sock must keep its shape when wet, keep you warm (or cool), and dry readily. The only real choice is wool or a wool-blend sock. And please don't protest that you can't wear wool next to your skin. Most who say that haven't even tried it, imagining wool to be itchy. The wool in socks is blended to be soft and smooth, and many socks today combine wool with some other moisture-hating fiber such as polypropylene or Hollofil, which increases their softness (and performance, in some respects).

Summer or winter, your socks should contain wool

Some folks are aghast at the thought of wearing wool in the summer. Yet when you examine the function of insulation, you realize it works to insulate from both cold and heat. But the most important aspect of wool or wool-blend socks is that perspiration (or water) is wicked away from your skin surface. By decreasing the amount of water next to your skin surface, the socks help the skin withstand friction, and this reduces greatly the chances of blisters. Cotton socks instead act as a sponge, retaining moisture.

If you don't believe me, why don't you run a test? Take a pair of each on your next trip and wear them alternately. I'm confident that most people will find wool more comfortable, more durable, better at absorbing shocks to the foot, and faster drying.

Underwear and extras

Wear what you want here, even if it has tiger strips or polka dots. Wear one, bring a change, just like your socks. T-shirts also make fine outerwear on hot days, and again, we wear one, pack another.

Long underwear does require a bit of discussion, though. It is your secret weapon to warmth with this layering system. Of critical importance is that long underwear tops and bottoms be made of a hydrophobic fabric such as polypropylene or Thermax since moisture next to your skin is the surest way to a chill, or even to hypothermia. Under the rest of your layers, these garments will add just the warmth you need in spring and fall; and if you purchase the light versions, such as runners or cross-country skiers wear, they are not too warm for the aerobic activity of portaging. They also add a great deal of comfort while you sleep on cold nights.

Mary Jo won't go on a canoe trip without her polypro top and bottom ever since an August canoe trip when the temperature dropped into the high twenties and the wind blew for days. Since she chills more easily than I, taking

Long underwear must wick water, not absorb it

polypro in the summer makes good sense. I sometimes leave mine at home, depending upon the forecast.

When you need this layer, long underwear could possibly be the most important item on this list.

Stuff a bandanna in your back pocket and you'll be glad you did. It will clean your glasses, serve as an impromptu wash-cloth, cool the back of your neck, or act as a hot-pad for handling steaming pots. You can even blow your nose in it. I once forgot mine and missed it badly the entire trip.

Swimsuits might be optional, depending on where you are heading and the nature of your group. We both use lightweight, quick-drying nylon athletic-type shorts. Mary Jo wears a T-shirt on top. The nice thing about using these items as swimwear is that they'll do double duty as shorts on hot days.

Cold weather clothing

When you're canoeing in the spring or fall, the weather can get pretty nippy here in Northern Minnesota. Perhaps I should even define these seasons for those of you from warmer climes. Well, the ice doesn't leave the lakes most years until May first, and no one who lives here is surprised by snow as late as the first week of June. Fall can begin in early September, and I've seen many years where it snowed by October. Granted, these early and late snowfalls usually don't add up to much, or stay on the ground long, but the cold air mass that brought them can stick around.

So, on a May or September canoe trip, and even into much of the summer, some type of insulating garment is often appropriate. In the summer it can be just a heavy wool shirt to throw on over your light shirt. Spring and fall might require something a bit warmer. Good choices are the polyester fleece jackets. Made from fabrics known as Polarfleece,

Polartec, Synchilla, and the like, they are wonderfully light and warm, won't absorb any water, and are launderable. Their only downfall is that sparks from the campfire will instantly melt a hole through them.

Some traditionalists still prefer wool because it won't easily burn and it is the best of all natural fabric materials at retaining warmth when wet. Although it isn't as good at this function as the polyester fleeces just mentioned, it certainly is adequate. Since cold weather and a dunking could lead to hypothermia, considering such an attribute is important. For that reason, cotton should be avoided. Sweatshirts and similar garments will actually suck heat from your body when they become wet.

I mentioned the long johns and stocking cap already, so only one possible item remains: gloves. In cold weather those who are susceptible to chilling should throw in a pair of gloves made of polyester fleece or wool. Be careful wearing polyester fleece gloves while cooking or stoking the fire because heat can melt the fabric, possibly causing burns to the wearer. Army surplus stores often sell ugly green wool liners for GI leather gloves. They are cheap and are great for camping.

Layering

Put as much of the above-mentioned stuff on as you need it to keep warm; peel down as you heat up. Except in the spring or fall, mostly what you'll end up packing are your changes of underwear and socks, maybe shorts or swimsuit, and possibly sneakers. If you are lucky, you'll be able to leave your rain gear packed the whole time, but don't count on it. Mary Jo and I once took a thirty-day canoe trip from late July to the end of August (we chose this time period for its consistently dry, warm weather) during which it rained for twenty-one days. Go figure.

One more thing: inquire how the rest of the members of

Your trip will be effected most by the person who is

❑ Least prepared

❑ Worst outfitted

❑ Most ill-clothed

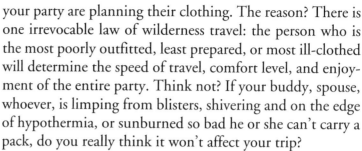

Repair kit

your party are planning their clothing. The reason? There is one irrevocable law of wilderness travel: the person who is the most poorly outfitted, least prepared, or most ill-clothed will determine the speed of travel, comfort level, and enjoyment of the entire party. Think not? If your buddy, spouse, whoever, is limping from blisters, shivering and on the edge of hypothermia, or sunburned so bad he or she can't carry a pack, do you really think it won't affect your trip?

Subdued colors are appropriate in a wilderness setting because they are less visible to other campers and therefore minimize the visual impact and sense of crowding.

Many folks get by without ever giving their clothing a second thought. Hooray for them. Luck can go a long way toward a successful wilderness visit. But certainly it doesn't hurt to give your clothing choices the same regard you should the rest of your equipment. And when the gods of wind and rain frown upon you, you can snicker back in relative comfort. It's a good feeling.

Your wilderness laundromat

Quality clothing shouldn't come apart on a canoe trip, but it doesn't hurt to be prepared to do a little mending. A button or two, a couple of safety pins, a needle and some thread will allow you to make needed repairs and won't take much space in your pack.

Should laundering be needed on a canoe trip, here's a simple tip. First, only a knothead does any washing in the canoe country's lakes and streams. It is unethical and causes pollution.

To do laundry, use a heavy-duty plastic bag (similar to your pack liner). Put some water (you can even use warm water if you like) in the bag (about 1/3 full), throw in some detergent (when we go on long trips and plan to do laundry we carry a little household laundry detergent; on short trips you'll only need to do socks, so the dish soap or face soap will do) and toss in the dirty clothes. Twist the bag's top, fold it over, and secure with a heavy rubber band. Put the bag on a smooth surface (a sleeping pad works nicely), grab the twisted top, and pump it up and down until your arm gets tired. The pumping provides similar agitation to that of a washing machine. Soon the water will be black. Now let it soak while you fish or pick blueberries.

Dump the dirty water at least 150 feet from the lake or stream. Put fresh water into the bag and run it through a rinse cycle (pumping again, but no soap). You might need to do this twice.

You'll be amazed at how clean your clothing is, and you did it all without polluting the lake or stream.

The Canoe Country Kitchen

I guess if you've ever seen how Charlie Brown's dog, Snoopy, behaves at dinner time, dancing his little doggy dance, you have a pretty fair idea of my behavior as our supper simmers. No doubt about it, meal time is a highly anticipated event during every canoe trip.

It can be a dreaded event as well, especially if the food is difficult to prepare, dull, or not filling enough. A bit of planning can help avoid the dreaded dinnertime blues.

So far in this book you've been subjected to my opinion on how many new products don't work as well as the old-fashioned items. Well, you won't read that in this chapter. Today's camper has an incredibly rich variety of foodstuffs from which to choose, some of them formulated specially for the camper, but much of them available directly from your supermarket shelves. And yes, we still have some traditional camping foods, like cheese or hard sausage, that haven't been improved upon and keep well on canoe trips.

Not only that, cooking has been made much easier with the wonderful camp stoves available today. No more fussing with a fire on wet days when trying to whip up a meal. Today's stoves are light, fast, and reliable.

Let's take a look at the many elements of canoe country cuisine and its preparation.

A bit of planning can help avoid the dreaded dinnertime blues

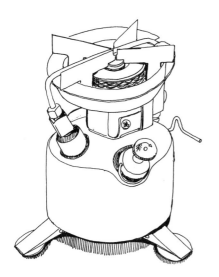

Sturdy single-burner stove

Equipment

While you certainly don't have to carry a stove, most folks I know won't go without one. A boon for cooking on wet days or for preparing a quick breakfast so you can get on your way early in the day, the lightweight backpacking stoves of today are wonders. Some campers consider them more environmentally sound than wood fires, and they certainly are in alpine settings. But the canoe country is full of downed wood for fuel, and it is an ever-renewing resource, unlike the petroleum from which stove fuel is refined. The real advantage of a stove in the north country is convenience.

There are a lot of stoves on the market. Important points to consider when purchasing one are the BTU output, time to bring water to a boil, fuel efficiency, and weight. I consider ease of operation and lack of fussiness also very important.

For that reason I would recommend any of the Coleman single-burner stoves. At the time of this writing, they have three backpacking stoves in their Peak 1 line, and each would be a fine choice. I don't hesitate to recommend these stoves over any other because they are incredibly reliable, durable, and simple to use, have wonderful flame adjustment, and perform well. They are also fuel-stingy. A full tank should last you for a weekend trip and an extra pint of fuel should be all you need on a four-day journey.

Extra fuel should be carried in a container specifically designed for that purpose. Some very nice light fuel bottles are being made out of aluminum or plastic in both half and full liter sizes.

I once had a stove that used an external fuel bottle and a little folding-legged burner. It sure threw the heat (about the same as a Peak 1) but lacked serious flame adjustment, required assembly every time it was used, and needed a ridiculous foil wind-screen to get decent performance. To top it off, in order to see the flame (for adjusting heat), you had to remove the windscreen. A pain to use.

Canister stoves that burn either propane or butane ought to be banned as far as I'm concerned. First, they don't perform nearly as well as a liquid-fuel stove, especially in cool weather. Second, manufacturing any product today with a short-lifespan throwaway metal fuel tank simply isn't environmentally responsible.

Some campers still use the bigger two-burner Coleman stoves that look like a small suitcase. These are particularly well-suited to large groups who base camp. They provide a wonderfully stable surface on which to cook larger, more elaborate meals. For groups who don't base camp and who'll be traveling nearly every day, these two-burners are simply too big and heavy. A better bet would be two single-burner stoves, which combined will weigh about seven pounds less than the big two-burner and take a quarter of the space. Two stoves aren't a necessity for larger groups, but you'll end up cooking and eating in shifts if you try to cook for everyone on just one burner.

Utensils for camping are simple: a knife, fork, and spoon per person and one spatula. Some campers like to add a large wooden spoon for stirring and serving. The nesting utensil sets sold at camping shops are just fine.

Cook kits are about the only other thing you'll need. The minimum you'll want is a two-quart pot, one plate and cup per person, and a fry pan. Forget those dinky little fry pans that come with most nesting cook kits and buy a ten-inch aluminum fry pan. Some nice ones with folding handles are made, or you can salvage an old one from home and remove the handle and then purchase an aluminum pot-lifter for use in the field. If you are traveling with a larger group, you'll probably need a pot larger than two quarts, perhaps as large as four quarts.

Many camping meals are one-pot affairs, so your pot will likely be the most-used item. Some campers prefer bowls to

Camp kitchen equipment

- ❏ Single-burner stove
- ❏ Plate, cup, knife, fork, spoon for each camper
- ❏ Spatula
- ❏ Large spoon
- ❏ Two-quart pot
- ❏ Ten-inch fry pan
- ❏ Coffee pot
- ❏ Pot lifter
- ❏ Scrub-up kit
- ❏ Spice-kit

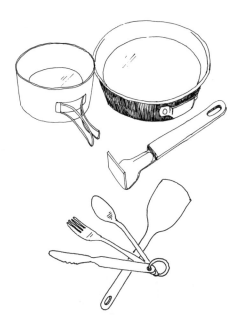

Cook kit and utensils

plates. If you eat a lot of oatmeal or one-pot meals, a bowl works just fine. But I've never liked the look of a crisp walleye fillet in a bowl, so we stick with plates. You can always use your mug anyway for foods like oatmeal.

In addition, you may want to consider an aluminum coffeepot. Even if you don't brew coffee, but prefer the instant version or tea, this pot comes in handy for such water-boiling chores. Ours is just large enough to hold our Peak 1 camp stove and weighs only a few ounces. It isn't an inconvenience to carry this pot even if it is used very little since it doesn't take up any more room in the pack than would the stove alone.

Coffee pot in cloth sack

If you cook on wood your pots and pans will get sooty. Some folks have a fetish about keeping their pots clean and spend an inordinate amount of time scrubbing. We simply constructed some cloth sacks that hold our well-blackened pots, thereby eliminating both the need to scour the outside and the soiling of other pack items that would be inevitable should a black pot come in contact with them. Our one- and two-quart nesting pots, with cups inside, go in one bag, the frying pan, with plates and utensils nested in it, is placed in another; and the coffee-pot/stove goes in a third.

Now you may wonder why not just buy one of those big cook kits that holds all of the above in one nesting package. I've always found that it is easier to pack an assortment of small items (this isn't limited to cooking gear) than one big thing of equal volume. The simple reason is that it is easier to work the individual items into the odd corners of the pack. Only when you travel with a party of six or more would those big cook kits really pay off in convenience.

Last on the list of cooking equipment comes the scrub-up kit and the spice kit. We use nylon ditty bags for each, the scrubbee and soap in a waterproof ditty bag and the spices in another.

Spice kit

Plastic 35mm film canisters are great for spices and some camping supply houses and catalogs sell snap-on shaker lids for them, which are wonderful. Spices will add very little weight to your food pack but can sure improve the flavor and looks of your dinner concoctions and are well worth carrying.

So that you don't end up with dish soap all over, put your liquid soap in a small, leakproof plastic camping bottle. Just take what you need, to avoid excess weight. We use regular, low-phosphate, liquid dish-washing detergent since we don't ever wash pots (or anything else) in the lakes or streams, and it works much better on greasy pots than the liquid "biodegradable" camp soap sold. I hate those soaps primarily because they imply that it is OK to wash in the lake. Regular detergent, when used well away from the water, breaks down quickly in the top inches of the soil.

Your menu will consist of items from the camper's four basic food groups: fresh meats and produce; supermarket prepared dinners; commercial freeze-dried or dehydrated camping foods; and wild foods (fish, berries, etc.). Each one of these groups does certain things well, and it would be foolish to limit your selection to just one group. Let's take a look at each.

Fresh foods

We often start our canoe trip with one meal of fresh foods for the first night out. It can be whatever you wish, but ours is usually some venison steak or chops sauteed with mushrooms and onions, a veggie of choice, and a side dish of noodles or rice. Meats should be well frozen before departure, with an additional wrapping of newspaper for insulation, and then placed in a sturdy plastic bag to avoid leakage. If they're frozen and kept out of the sun, you might be able to extend the shelf (pack?) life of fresh meats for up to three days. But since they are heavy and bulky, we rarely use them past the first day. Fresh vegetables will keep for three or four days easily, but

Four basic food groups for campers

❏ Fresh meats and produce

❏ Supermarket prepared meals

❏ Commercial camping foods

❏ Wild foods

Fresh foods from the market

Fresh foods keep well for the first days out

- ❏ Vegetables
- ❏ Breads
- ❏ Crackers
- ❏ Cheese
- ❏ Dry sausage
- ❏ Eggs

again, space and weight begin to be factors. I've seen folks carrying corn on the cob, sacks of potatoes and bunches of onions. Tasty, but definitely very heavy.

Other fresh foods that keep well are breads (although they squash easily!), most cheeses, and some smoked meats. Some types of hard crackers are good substitutes for bread, and they keep indefinitely provided you don't turn them to sawdust by mashing them. Eggs also keep very well, up to four or five days when kept out of the sun. We put ours in a plastic egg container made for camping, and this has worked well. Just to be safe, though, we always place the container in a plastic bag.

Although it seems like it should be the other way around, low-fat cheese doesn't hold up as well as regular cheese. On a warm day low-fat cheese gets very runny and messy. You're going to be burning up a lot of calories, so go with the high-fat stuff. It keeps better too.

True dry salamis and other dry sausage will keep almost forever. Unfortunately they are hard to find. If the sausage you buy is stored in the market's cooler, figure it will last only three or four days. The real dry sausage will be kept at room temperature and is usually characterized by a white-powdered surface. This is the preferred item for long trips.

Bacon is similar. The stuff in the shrink-wrapped packaging has about the same life expectancy as most sausage—a few days. If you can find a butcher shop that smokes their own, and you can get them to sell you a pound on the rind (unsliced with heavy, smokey crust on the outside) you're in luck. We've found this to keep over a week, even in August. However, use your head with any fresh food. If it begins to smell weird or develops a slightly slimy coating, don't eat it.

Margarine keeps better than butter. Cooking oil lasts almost forever. Put these in leakproof Nalgene (best brand of plastic camping containers) bottles or tubs. Syrup usually comes in a plastic squeeze bottle right from the supermarket, and since this container is burnable, technically it is legal in the BWCAW and Quetico. We usually transfer syrup, though, to a smaller reusable camping squeeze bottle so we aren't carrying an excess amount. Remember—no food-stuffs or drinks may be taken into the BWCAW or Quetico in cans or bottles unless the containers are reusable or burnable.

What about coolers? Some folks do use them, but generally they are a considerable waste of space and weight. Hard-sided coolers are a nuisance on portages, and unless you've had a special pack constructed to fit them, difficult to get in a pack. We have tried some of the new fabric coolers that use foam or Thinsulate for insulation and found that they work quite well. But since we rarely take foods that need refrigeration except for use within the first forty-eight hours, and since they'll keep just fine until then without the cooler, we have quit using even the fabric coolers. If you place your frozen or well-chilled items in the center of your food pack, the other items snuggled around them will provide some insulation. We've often found our frozen meats still require some thawing, even on the second day.

Supermarket foods

The supermarket shelves these days hold so many foods that lend themselves to camping that it is entirely possible to outfit your camping food needs without ever buying a specialized camping food item. I enjoy stalking the isles of supermarkets reading prepared-food labels to see if the item is suitable for field use. Some things to consider when examining these meals are added extra ingredients needed (milk, margarine, etc.) and cooking time.

You'll find that many types of noodle, rice, or potato side dishes are very suitable for camping and make a fine base from which to construct a whole meal. If the label calls for the addition of milk, don't despair. Most will be fine if you only add water or do what we do, add water and throw

Packaged foods from the market

Supermarket foods add variety to your menus

- ❏ Prepared noodle, rice or potato dinners
- ❏ Soup mix
- ❏ Pasta salad
- ❏ Pancake and biscuit mix
- ❏ Instant oatmeal
- ❏ Dried fruit
- ❏ Instant coffee
- ❏ Dry milk
- ❏ Tea
- ❏ Cocoa
- ❏ Hard candy
- ❏ Presweetened Kool-Aid
- ❏ No-bake desserts

in some powdered milk. Consider the cooking time too. If it takes thirty minutes of simmering, you'll consume too much fuel. Even if you're cooking on wood, such an amount of fire wood is time consuming to gather. Many of these products cook in only ten to fifteen minutes.

We commonly start with a packaged noodle dinner and prepare it according to the instructions, but slightly increase the water or milk content. Then we toss in some freeze-dried (or fresh) vegetables and some freeze-dried meat and allow it all to cook for the specified time. A meal like this is relatively inexpensive and satisfies the two of us. If we've been fortunate enough to catch a few fish, we eliminate the freeze dried meat, cook the noodle dinner as a side dish, and prepare the veggies separately.

Many prepared dinners are usable in this manner. Oriental-style ramen soups, with the water content cut in half, form a very inexpensive base for these kinds of dinners. Some other products we've found that work nicely are the various flavored rice dishes, a variety of dried potato products, and pasta salads that come complete with a sealed package of mayonnaise. A little pepperoni cut up and mixed with a cool pasta salad, on hot summer days when you can't bear the thought of a warm meal, is a real treat. Check out the oriental grocery if you have one in your town. We've found many interesting dried products there that work well for camping. Our favorite has been dried shrimp—absolutely wonderful in a pasta salad.

You'll find other useful items in your supermarket as well: add-water-only pancake and biscuit mixes, dried soups, instant oatmeal, granola bars, and dried fruits. Pick up some peanuts, raisins, and M&Ms and make yourself a bag of gorp. Instant coffee, tea, cocoa, hard candies, and Kool-Aid drink mixes (presweetened) can round out your larder. Even the dried beef that comes in a little jar works well. Just make sure you put it in a plastic bag and leave the jar at home.

Finally, you can even find no-bake chocolate cake or

cheesecake on the shelves. These and other no-bake desserts work very nicely in the field.

Explore your supermarket with camping on your mind. You'll be surprised how much you'll find.

Commercial camping foods

Should you wish to take the easy way out, you can simply wander down to your camping store and buy some of the wonderful trail foods that are on the market today. They are quick, easy to make, and very tasty. But they are kind of expensive.

These foods are broken down into *no cook* and *quick cook* products. Primarily, the former are freeze-dried foods that require only immersion in hot water and the latter require some soaking and cooking time. A wide range of breakfast, supper, and dessert items are available.

Some caution is warranted when planning your menu with these foods. A package that says *serves two* will do so only if it is part of the meal, not the whole meal. A few years ago I wrote a review of camp foods for a magazine. I asked each of the major camp food manufacturers to send me what they considered an adequate menu for two people on a four-day canoe trip. With one exception, we received meals that were pretty complex. For instance, a dinner would consist of a soup mix, a *serves two* entree such as beef stroganoff, a drink mix, and some type of dessert. And by and large, it took all these items to satisfy our hunger. If you were to purchase only the entree, figuring it would fill two weary campers, you'd be very disappointed. If you do plan to utilize only the entrees, plan on one *serves two* package per person. You can save a little money by purchasing a *serves four* entree for every two campers.

There are differences between the major brands of camping foods, usually in portion size. If two stroganoff dinners boast twenty-four ounces of cooked product, but one brand

Portion sizes on packaged foods are usually inadequate if you are planning a one-dish meal

Freeze-dried foods

Freeze-dried meats and vegetables add variety and nutrition to packaged entrees from the supermarket

weighs six ounces dry and the other eight, the only way they can be equal at the end is that one requires more water. In other words, it will have less food value. Similarly, the real measurement of camping foods is the carbohydrates and calories yielded. We're not on a diet out there, folks. The brand that delivers the greatest number of carbos, as well as calories, will provide you with the most fuel and leave you with a full feeling. There can be a surprising difference between brands in these categories. Unfortunately, not much of this information is printed on the label, but it is generally available from the manufacturer if you request it. We have found that Harvest Foodworks brand products consistently have adequate portion sizes and caloric value, and are also tasty. In fact, these are the only meals I know of that meet this standard: when they say a dinner will feed two, you can rely upon it and carry only one package per two people.

We generally carry one or two commercial camping dinners on every canoe trip for those occasions when we are too pooped out to cook or the weather is unbearably bad. Since all you have to do is heat water, these meals work well for these situations. Sometimes we add a special breakfast from these lines of foods as well for a treat on layover days. Generally, we don't do much cooking for breakfast because, with just the two of us, it takes too much time on travel days to prepare an elaborate breakfast and then wash up. For those days we simply have a cup of instant coffee or tea, some instant oatmeal or granola bars and then break camp. Save big breakfasts for layover days, or for when you are traveling in large groups where a designated cook can take care of the chores while everyone else breaks camp.

I'd warrant we use more of the freeze-dried meats and vegetables than we do any of the entrees. Added to a supermarket noodle or rice dinner, a two-ounce package of meat and the same size envelope of veggies will make a hearty and fairly inexpensive one-pot dinner.

When you do purchase a camping entree, why not try

something exotic. An enchilada or oriental-style meal after a few days of noodles is a real treat!

Wild foods

One reason we don't carry much meat is that there's plenty of protein to be had where we're going: fish. The Quetico and Boundary Waters lakes provide not only the opportunity for great paddling and scenery but sometimes fabulous fishing. Occasionally we invite a fish or two back to camp to join us for dinner.

A fish dinner is great but don't count on always finding cooperative fish

Just be certain you never count on a fish dinner. You should always have a back-up meal in mind in case the weather or fish don't cooperate. But to avoid carrying a lot of extra food, we plan a fish dinner with a noodle side dish as well as some freeze-dried vegetables. We carry an extra package of freeze-dried meat just in case. If you catch fish, great. Just save the dried meat for another time. If the fish elude you, throw the meat, veggies, and noodles into one pot and go to it.

Cooking fish is simple, and frying is probably the most popular way. You'll need a little cooking oil and some kind of coating mix for the fish. Commercial fish batters are on the market, or you can use any type of flour, pancake, or biscuit mix. We carry a plastic sack of cornflake crumbs, to which we have added Cajun seasonings combined with some Lawry's season salt. Adding favorite spices to your coating mix at home saves a step in the field. Just throw the washed fillets into the coating mix sack, shake until coated, and then into the oil they go. Fish should be cooked very quickly in almost smoking oil. Only a couple of minutes per side and the fillets will be done.

You can also cook fish by boiling. Lake trout lends itself nicely to this method because it is oily enough to survive the dunking. Just gut and clean the trout (no need to scale lake trout), cut it into steaks (1 1/2-inch-wide chunks, through

Foods from field and stream

the backbone) and toss them into boiling water to which you've added some salt (a big tablespoon) and spices (peppercorns and a bay leaf are nice). Boil for about five minutes, remove, and then just pick the meat off the bones and skin and dip in melted butter or margarine. If you are preparing a soup, filleted chunks of fish can be added to make a chowder as well.

Come July and August, if the weather has been favorable, the canoe country is lush with both blueberries and, in old clearings and burns, raspberries. Added to your pancakes or bannock, they can make an everyday meal taste like a special occasion.

Bannock, by the way, is the fry bread that was a staple for old woodsmen and Indians. A lot of folks do some pretty elaborate baking on canoe trips, usually with a folding reflector oven. This is an enjoyable pastime in itself, but should really be limited to base camping. If you are planning on covering some distance on your trip, moving just about every day, a reflector oven is just something else to lug around. You can make delicious bannock in the frying pan already included in your cook kit.

Bannock can be as simple as flour, water, baking powder and salt. Our recipe, making enough for the two of us, contains two cups flour, two teaspoons baking powder, 1/2 teaspoon salt, and just enough water to make a firm dough. Mix the dry ingredients together at home and put in a plastic bag. You can add a little dried egg and a tablespoon of cooking oil if you wish. Adding a little water at a time, knead the dough into a one inch thick cake, working quickly. The baking powder releases gas, which causes the bread to rise while cooking. Overworking the dough releases this gas prematurely.

Grease your frying pan, put the cake in it, and set it above the fire until a bottom crust forms. Once the cake is browned on the bottom, remove the pan from above the fire, prop it as nearly upright as possible a foot or so from the

Bannock for two

2 cups flour

2 tsp. baking powder

1/2 tsp. salt

water

Options: dried egg, oil, sugar

blueberries or raspberries

fire, and let it bake until done (when the top is brown). Add fresh blueberries and some sugar to the dough before baking for a real treat. Or to make a breakfast coffee cake, mix in cinnamon and sugar. Served hot with some margarine or butter, it won't last long, I guarantee.

For those of you who are knowledgeable about mushrooms, you'll find edible varieties in the North Woods. I can recognize with certainty only puffballs and morels. If you have no idea if a mushroom is safe to eat, assume they are poisonous. To do otherwise could be fatal.

Crawfish can make a tasty meal if you are willing to go to the work of gathering enough to bother cooking. These little lobsters are abundant in the canoe country and are cooked the same way as their saltwater cousins—in boiling water. You'll need about thirty, though, to satisfy two people.

Menu planning

Menu planning is an art that can be mastered only with time afield. The goal is to carry just enough food to last the trip and no more. Your food pack should be nearly empty when you leave.

For me to advise you how much food to take is difficult since everyone's appetite is so very different. But you can narrow things down at home. In fact, it is critical that you do so. When planning your trip with your crew, ask each one about food preferences and appetite. You don't want to plan oatmeal for breakfast each day only to find out old Fred won't eat it, and then have him dip into your carefully planned lunch menu to satisfy his hunger.

I can give you some guidelines, however. Two and one-half pounds of food per person per day is an old standard formula that still works well, despite the new lighter dried foods. Why? Well, the addition of fresh foods for the first few days, and heavy things like nuts, granola bars, and the like, will make up for the weight saving from dried dinners.

Check out food likes and dislikes before you begin to plan menus

This total weight will also include foodstuffs such as oil, margarine, and flour.

Now obviously you're not going to weigh each person's portion of oil for each day. The point is that if the total weight of the food equals 2 1/2 pounds, times the number of people, times the number of days, you'll know that you're on the right track.

Aside from some trail snacks such as gorp (good old raisins & peanuts), dried fruits, or granola bars, the three main meals are all that you'll eat. Impress that on your party members. Some who say they aren't big eaters really are, but are used to grazing all day long while at home. That simply won't work on a canoe trip. There's no fridge in the campsite to peruse before bedtime to satisfy a latent hunger.

The real difficulty lies in determining portion size per person, and that depends very much on what kind of meal you prepare. As mentioned earlier, with the exception of Harvest Foodworks meals, commercial freeze-dried dinner entrees are designed to be eaten with soups, desserts, and so on. If you rely solely upon the entree, plan on one "Serves Two" package per person.

Supermarket foods such as Lipton noodle dishes should be used with the following plan: as a side dish with fish, one package per two people; as the main course with added freeze dried veggies (2-ounce package per package of noodles or rice) and dried meat or sausage, one noodle package per two people will be sufficient, but may leave big eaters a tad hungry. When using ramen noodles, figure one package per person. It is a good idea to prepare some of these meals at home in advance so you have an idea of how large the servings are and if you feel full after eating them.

Measure margarine, oil, flour, etc., carefully. Look at the cooking instructions on food packages. If each noodle dinner calls for two tablespoons of margarine and a cup of milk, then take only the appropriate amount of each (substituting dried milk). Planning carefully will help eliminate a lot of needless weight and waste. Leftovers after a meal are always a problem in the wilderness. If you dump it in the woods, or even bury it, it attracts insects and bears. You can build a hot fire and burn it, but what do you do on wet days? About the only real recourse, other than careful planning to eliminate leftovers, is to have a teenager in the party. Then there won't be any leftovers.

Here are a few more general guidelines, all based on a two-person serving for one meal: bacon, 1/2 lb.; cheese and salami for lunch, 1/2 lb. per day; fresh eggs, two per person per meal; Granola bars (when used extensively as trail snacks or quick breakfasts), minimum of six per person per day; oatmeal, approximately 1/2 cup per person per meal; drink mixes such as Kool-Aid, enough to make one quart per two people per meal.

Finally, you need to select condiments and odds and ends such as nuts, dried fruits, seasonings, and the like. The only way I know to determine how much to pack is to figure exactly when that item is to be consumed (for example, dried fruit in oatmeal, third day), set aside what I would consider a fair serving, and then multiply that times the number of folks. Not very scientific, maybe, but the method works well. After a few trips, you'll simply be able to bag up these items with just a nod to measurements.

Packing the Food Pack

Your food pack will likely be the heaviest pack of the bunch. Be careful not to make it so heavy no one can carry it or so heavy you have difficulty hanging it to avoid bear problems. I prefer to carry two smaller food packs on long trips, or with big groups, so that each is manageable. Mary Jo and I once filled a huge pack with food for a very long canoe trip and only realized what a monster the thing was to hang or move after the float-plane dropped us off and was winging its way south. I've never made that mistake again.

Watch the weight of the food pack—someone will have to carry it, full, across that first portage

83

You can use a standard #3 Duluth Pack for a food pack, or purchase one of the special packs made for this purpose. Specialty packs are usually small and more rectangular to allow for a rigid cardboard box to be slipped inside (although the #3 pack will accommodate a box as well). The advantage of a box in the pack is that it helps to protect the food and gives the pack some shape, which prevents hard items from boring into your back while you're portaging and makes it a lot easier to rummage through the pack in search of something.

I prefer a Cruiser Combo pack, made by Duluth Tent and Awning, mentioned already in the equipment chapter. This is nothing more than the venerable old #2 Cruiser pack (with side pockets added) slipped over an ash pack basket. The basket takes the place of the box and lasts for years, and we find that this size provides ample storage for the two of us for a seven-to-ten-day trip. They also make a larger #3 Cruiser Combo. The side pockets are really a handy feature because they allow you to keep the day's lunch items, water bottle, and some trail snacks accessible.

Whatever you use, first line the pack with a heavy plastic bag and then insert the box or basket. When preparing foods for the trail, remove any excess packaging such as boxes (but remember to save the instructions!) and place items in plastic bags. A real handy way of keeping track of your meals is to combine all the ingredients for a particular meal in one bag. For instance, one package of Lipton noodles, one pack freeze-dried meat, one pack freeze-dried veggies and a little sack of powdered milk all goes into one bag or can be made into one bundle with masking tape. On the tape write: Dinner - day 2. Now when you start to cook all you need is to grab the one package instead of rummaging all through the pack. Bundling foods this way also aids in menu planning, because you can see at a glance if you have what you need and in what amounts.

Try to keep crushable items near the top of the pack.

A "Dinner-day 2" bag

- ❑ 1 package Lipton noodles
- ❑ 1 pack freeze-dried meat
- ❑ 1 pack freeze-dried veggies
- ❑ 1 small sack powdered milk

Make sure that everything is well sealed. The interior plastic bags, as well as the heavy plastic liner, not only keep the food protected from moisture, but help to contain spills and, most important, reduce food odors, which are bound to attract bears.

Fresh or frozen foods should be stored in the refrigerator until just before departure and then placed into the pack. If you have a long drive to your entry point, put perishables and frozen foods in a cooler for the trip and then transfer them to the food pack at the last moment. Don't trust grocery store wrappings on meats, cheeses, sausage, and such. They'll leak for sure unless placed in another bag. As I mentioned before, plastic egg containers made for camping work well, or you can take a standard egg carton, shape some heavy corrugated cardboard around it, and seal it with duct tape. This works pretty well and has the advantage of being burnable, thereby saving space in the food pack.

Put liquids, peanut butter, jelly, margarine, and similar goopy things into reusable plastic tubs or bottles to avoid leaky messes in your food pack.

Well-planned meals are a real boon to the quality of your canoe trip. You may make a wide range of choices as to what to eat, but the challenge is the same for all of us: good variety, palatability, ease of cooking, and minimal storage size and weight. Take what you want; just make sure you have meals that will be something to look forward to, not something to dread. Oh yeah, make sure you can lift the pack off the floor, too.

Snacks to keep you going

Find yourself getting cranky after a few hours of paddling and portaging? Do you run out of steam part way through long portages? If so, eat something.

It is critical that you keep your body fueled under the exertion experienced on canoe trips. Often, all you need is a

Trail mix

1 box of raisins

1 can of peanuts

1 large bag of M&M's

handful of gorp or a granola bar to lift your spirits and restore your blood sugar level. It's not a bad idea, at the beginning of each day, to hand out a couple of granola bars or other snacks to each individual so that they can put them in their pockets to have on hand when they begin to tucker out. It doesn't do much good if the food pack is in the other canoe or at the far end of the portage when the poor soul runs out of gas.

Knowing we have a difficult, windy stretch of water to cross or a long portage to endure, we often stop first for a quick snack before tackling the task. Doing this, or taking short food breaks regularly, will greatly increase your ability to travel efficiently and far. A leisurely lunch break half-way through the day, with enough time for a quick snooze, can double the distance you might have traveled if you had simply pushed on in a tired trudge. It is critical as well to drink plenty of fluids.

Pay attention to what your body needs for fluids and fuel and you'll be surprised how much more easily the difficult tasks fall.

Packing for the Portage

The sleekness of your canoe won't determine how far you travel. The sophistication of your paddles and technique won't define how fast you go. Even your most fervent wishes and careful planning won't put you at your secret camp of solitude or that remote fishing hole. More than any other factor on your canoe trip, it will be how you handle the portages that controls ease, speed, and distance.

And how you pack governs how you portage.

There are two common dictums concerning canoe trips. The first is that you need not worry too much about weight since the canoe carries the load. Second, you can always double portage. The first is blatantly incorrect and the second, though true, will increase your toil and decrease your efficiency.

Obviously, the first argument goes right out the window as soon as you hit the landing at the first portage. You indeed will carry the load—all of it, including the canoe—overland. And as I said before, there is no such thing as a double portage. Walking back to retrieve that second load constitutes a trip in itself, totaling three.

If you recall, in the first chapter I gave you a formula for estimating travel time. Because double portaging actually triples the time it takes to get your gear across a portage, you can use that formula to see just how much time you can save

To go farther, faster, and with greater ease—single portage . . . to single portage—pack light and pack well

Portage times

If it takes one hour to single portage, it takes three hours (across, back, across again) to double portage

by single portaging. Not only can you penetrate farther into the wilderness than you ever have before, but you'll also be able to reach your old favorite spots in about half the time you did previously. I know of no other way to make your canoe trip more efficient than by paying attention to how you pack.

Before we press on, however, let me give you a tip on how you can save time even if you choose not to single portage. Rather than take one load all the way across the portage, then return for the remainder, it is more efficient to "hopscotch" or "leapfrog" the loads over land. Grab your canoe and pack, carry both as far as you can, drop one, and continue with the other. When you get tired, put that load down and return for the half you left behind. Grab that, carry it an equal distance past where you dropped the second load, leave it, and return again. In this manner you rest during the short return walks and save some time. We often do this on very long trips, when our heavy food load simply doesn't allow for a single trip across the portage.

The single portage requires planning. There can be few or no loose items. We've all seen folks with heaps of fishing rods, landing nets, tackle boxes, and who-knows-what all strewn about at the portage landing. You'd have to be built with the appendages of an octopus to get that stuff across in a single trip. What can't be stored in your packs should be lashed into the canoe, with the exception of life jackets and paddles, which can then be easily handled. What remains, then, must be in Duluth Packs, two to be exact (for two people)—one for food and one for gear. On normal four-day canoe trips, larger groups can usually still get by with one food pack, but the equipment packs will increase in number. Generally, though, unless you haul a bunch of needless junk, you should be able to get by with one gear pack per two people, an amount that will still allow for single portaging if a couple of the party members are willing to double up with two packs or a pack and canoe.

Yes, light, easy travel does involve leaving extra toys at home. And it surely involves careful planning.

And yes, it means that someone must carry a canoe and a pack (or two packs) at the same time, which makes some folks shudder at the thought. But what I have noticed is that there really isn't much difference in effort or discomfort in carrying both if you are careful to keep the pack weight around thirty pounds (or less). Most of us can negotiate a portage without exhaustion. The discomfort is usually in the shoulders, and that pain is primarily from the weight of the canoe. In other words, the shoulders give out before the legs do, and so carrying a light pack doesn't greatly contribute to that discomfort. If you can carry a canoe across a portage, you can do it while wearing a pack of reasonable weight. Trust me.

Planning for the single portage

If you've read the earlier chapters, and not just skipped to this one first (shame on you), you've noticed I've been paying pretty strict attention to the weight of some items. That is because it isn't easy to hit that twenty-five to thirty-five pound gear pack weight without counting ounces. Just think, if your tent weighs twelve pounds, well, you're already halfway to the limit. And the goal isn't to see who can get to the limit first.

When Mary Jo and I travel, our gear pack contains everything that is not food or not for cooking. That means we try to include our cook kit and stove in the food pack. We don't want food odors mingling with our sleeping bags or clothing. On some occasions, though, we may have to make an exception to save room in the food pack for more chow, so we put the cook kit or stove (or both) into the gear pack. After the food begins to dwindle, however, we return these items to the food pack. As the trip wears on, you can add even more things to the food pack to make the canoe carrier's job easier and to make the load sharing a bit more

The gear pack holds:

- ❏ Tent
- ❏ Ground cloth
- ❏ Nylon tarp
- ❏ Sleeping bags
- ❏ Foam pads
- ❏ Clothing
- ❏ Rain gear
- ❏ Flashlight
- ❏ Rope
- ❏ Parachute cord X
- ❏ Folding saw X
- ❏ First aid kit
- ❏ Trowel (Quetico only, for digging latrine)
- ❏ Fire grate (Quetico only, for cooking over wood)
- ❏ Toilet paper X
- ❏ Toiletries
- ❏ Repair kit (duct tape, sewing kit)
- ❏ Sponge (for bailing canoe)

fair. It is safe to put fishing tackle, ropes, and such, into the food pack, but never stuff your sleeping bag or tent into the food pack unless it is totally sealed by plastic. You certainly don't want a bear to take a liking to your tent or sleeping bag because it smells like bacon and chocolate.

Now this two-pack rule is a hard one to follow, I'll admit that. We do sometimes fudge by carrying a small "overflow" daypack, for items such as my camera gear, fishing tackle, and the like. Mostly this occurs on spring or fall trips, when the main gear pack is stuffed to the brim with thicker sleeping bags and warmer clothes. As long as we are carrying this third cheater pack, we'll also put our rain gear or other light items in it. Notice I said light, because whoever is carrying the food pack will also have to carry this pack.

If you'll look at the equipment checklist elsewhere in this chapter, you'll notice that there isn't much left to cram in the gear pack. Aside from miscellaneous items, the biggest bulk comes from the tent, sleeping bags, foam pads, spare clothing, and, perhaps, cooking gear. All of this will fit in a #3 Duluth Pack.

If the weight of your equipment is first on the list in importance, size is certainly a close second. And it is the size of your sleeping bags that is most critical. They are generally the bulkiest items you'll carry. We discussed sleeping bags in the chapter on equipment, and you'll remember I suggested using summer-weight synthetic or down bags, along with compression stuff sacks. We get both of our thirty-degree down bags into one compression stuff sack. You'll need one compression sack for each synthetic summer-weight bag.

This is the heart and soul of fitting all your gear in a minimum of packs, because a pair of three-season synthetic-fill bags stuffed into a normal stuff sack will very nearly fill a pack. Believe me, once you've switched to light bags and compression sacks, you'll wonder how you got along without them.

Select all the rest of your equipment, such as tents and foam pads, with an eye toward weight and size. Keep extra clothing to a minimum. Except for spare clothes, what you take on a four-day canoe trip and what gear you pack for a twenty-day adventure remains pretty much the same. After all, once you've boiled your equipment choices down to the bare necessities, there isn't much room to subtract, nor much need to add. Once you trim your main equipment needs to include items of only reasonable weight and size, you'll have plenty of room in your pack for the various other small items that you'll want or need: first aid kit, paperback novel, flashlight, and such.

Packing the pack

All canoe packs are best packed by first placing the pack on a flat surface, shoulder straps down, with the opening of the pack toward you. Loading a pack in this manner allows for more careful placement of items along the back of the pack without fighting gravity. It is important to do it in this manner so that hard or knobby items aren't placed against the side of the pack that will be against your back. Nothing is more uncomfortable than to find that there is a coffeepot spout seeking your spine.

First, line the pack with a heavy-duty polyethylene bag of at least six-mil thickness to make the pack waterproof. These bags are available from most outfitters, from some outing shops, and by mail from Duluth Tent and Awning. Obtain these heavy-duty liners if at all possible, because they are much more durable than plastic trash sacks. If you are forced to use plastic trash sacks, use at least two, one inside the other. Please pay attention to this process, because it is the cornerstone of keeping your equipment dry.

Some canoeing books recommend further use of plastic bags for each item but we have never found this necessary as long as you use a heavy liner and take care not to puncture it.

The food pack holds:

❏ Food

The gear or food pack (whichever has space) holds:

❏ Cook kit
❏ Utensils
❏ Stove
❏ Stove fuel
❏ Dish soap / scrubbee
❏ Water bottle
❏ Water sack ✗

Day packs and pockets hold:

❏ Matches
❏ Bug dope
❏ Compass
❏ Map
❏ Camera
❏ Fishing gear ✗
  telephone

Tuck small items in the gear pack

Heavy plastic pack liners are
essential to keep gear and
food dry

The six-mil liners are plenty tough, and we have sometimes managed to use the same one for a whole summer. Inspect it occasionally by removing the liner from your pack and holding it up to the light. If you spot a hole, you can repair liners in the field by sandwiching any holes between two layers of duct tape or the waterproof adhesive tape from your first aid kit.

For typical Boundary Waters and Quetico canoe camping, this amount of waterproofing is sufficient. When the pack is fully loaded and the liner is rolled down and secured under the tight straps of the pack's flap, no water will reach your equipment. In fact, a pack so waterproofed will float almost indefinitely should the unfortunate happen and you swamp your canoe. Whitewater canoeists frequently lash their packs into the canoe so that the packs displace water that might enter the boat while at the same time offering floatation. If not lashed in, the packs would simply bob up out of a swamped canoe and float away. Occasionally you see folks lashing packs into the canoe even on flatwater trips such as those you'll be taking. Though such a precaution can't hurt, it is largely unnecessary in the canoe country. We do it only when crossing large lakes with rough seas. To do so under more ideal conditions only slows you down each time you land at or leave a portage.

After placing the liner in the pack, start by loading items into what would be the bottom of the pack if it were standing. Choose long, lightweight objects first, such as your foam pad. Remember, the heaviest items to be packed should always be near the pack's top. This ensures a center of gravity that stays near your own. Bottom-heavy packs pull down and away from you, forcing you to lean forward to counterbalance the load.

With the foam pad(s) widthwise in the pack's bottom, place similar long, slender items, such as your sleeping bags in compression sacks, in next. Your pack should now be about one-third full. At this point fold flat any tarps, jackets, and such, and use them as padding against the remaining exposed back area of the pack. Next you can load your spare clothing, toiletries, cook kit, and so on into the pack.

You can now stand the pack up and gently force the contents down into the pack. Remaining gear can be put in any way it best fits, taking care that hard items are kept away from the side facing your back, or that they are well padded by the folded tarp or jackets. Usually, tent poles, folding saws, and other slender items can be slid down the edge of the pack, generally between the liner bag and pack. Be careful not to puncture the liner. If you fold and roll your tent carefully so that it fits the width of your pack, you can place that at or near the top of the pack. Since it is your heaviest single item, the tent should go on top to keep the pack in balance. This placement is also a blessing if you are forced to set up camp in the rain, allowing you to get at it easily without exposing the rest of your gear to moisture.

You'll still have a lot of space in the pack for the remaining small items: paperback novel, journal, the oh-so-important toilet paper. These can be slid in to fill the odd nooks and crannies. The Duluth Pack is an amazing thing, and with some judicious squeezing and cramming, there almost always seems to be room for one more small item. It is really a handy trick to place many of these things in nylon ditty bags. We have all of our toiletries in one; another is our camping version of the household "junk" drawer that contains extra matches, a sewing kit, clothes pins, and so on. Each ditty bag is a different color so that we can readily identify the contents. Ditty bags make finding these things a much simpler task.

With the pack full, roll down the liner and gently squash the whole load down. Rain gear is best placed on top of the liner so that it is easily reached. Close the pack's top flap and fasten the straps. Now put the pack horizontally on the ground again, and with your hands and knees, shape and knead the pack until you have a tight square package, the

Packing order

❏ Light at the bottom

❏ Heavy at the top

❏ Soft next to your body

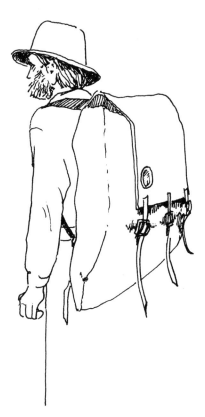

Pack rides high on back

sign of a seasoned voyageur. Readjust the flap straps now if needed.

A word about shoulder straps. On any pack that doesn't have a hip belt, it is very important to keep the shoulder straps as tight as possible. If your pack pulls painfully at your shoulders, I'd be willing to bet that the shoulder straps are too loose, allowing the pack to sag backward and down. A pack must ride tight to the body. Some packs have a quick-adjust feature to the shoulder straps that allows you to tighten them after the pack is on your back. Simply hunch your shoulders up very quickly and then bend forward to keep the weight high on your back while tugging down on the adjustment tabs. When you stand upright, the pack will remain high and tight to your back. With more traditional canoe packs with a buckle and roller system on the straps, you'll want to adjust the straps permanently to fit you, because it is nearly impossible to do so with the pack on. The straps should be only loose enough for you to just get your arms through them when mounting the pack.

Practice packing and adjusting your pack at home. Since your equipment is bound to be different than ours, and pack sizes vary, you'll need to experiment a bit to find the best method for you. Much better doing this in your living room than on some insect-infested canoe landing.

Whenever you lift and move canoe packs, as in loading and unloading a canoe, the best method is to grab the pack by the "ears" (the outside top edge of the flap) and then lift. It saves wear and tear on straps and the pack hangs vertically, making precise placement in the canoe easier.

Everything in its place

With your gear pack neatly stuffed and the food pack ready to go, there will inevitably be some odd items that fit no place very well. Bug dope can be stuffed into pants or shirt pocket. The map can be jammed under a pack's top flap. The water bottle can be placed in the food pack's side pocket, if it has one.

You may, however, want to keep some items near at hand—sunscreen, bird identification book, your camera. As I mentioned earlier, you can add a small daypack just for such things without compromising your ability to single portage. Actually, the weight of this pack is more important than size, but I keep emphasizing a small pack for the simple reason that a pack inevitably gets filled to its carrying capacity (and then some). Though your best intentions are to keep only a few things in that medium-size pack, it will, I guarantee, find itself home to items you would have otherwise left at home, making it much more of a burden for someone to carry. Keep in mind that whoever is carrying the canoe will also carry the gear pack, and the second person will carry the food pack as well as this daypack. Some portagers throw the small pack on top of the main pack and keep it there with one hand. Others prefer to carry the second pack by wearing it on the chest. Whichever way you choose, the smaller and lighter the pack, the better.

Of all the items you'll carry, few are more susceptible to damage from hard knocks and water than your camera gear. Small "point and shoot" cameras can be carried in a zipper-lock bag, protected from bumps by wrapping it in a shirt or jacket, and then placed in a pack. Full-sized 35mm gear is a bit harder to protect. You can wrap this equipment in plastic and place it in your gear pack, but you sure won't take many photos; retrieving the camera will be such an inconvenience you'll simply pass up many photo opportunities. You can also invest in a rigid, waterproof camera case. These, however, won't fit in packs and are a nuisance on the canoe country's frequent portages. While the camera will certainly be protected, again, the cumbersome case will dissuade you from shooting many photos.

Camera fits in daypack

I'll admit that finding a system for the avid photographer to use on a canoe trip is a balance between gear protection and ease of accessibility. The only sure way to come home with photos that you'll be proud of is to take plenty of them, and you just won't do so if your camera is hard to get to. Since photography is a part of my livelihood, I insist on having the camera near at hand, and so sacrifice camera protection for ease of access. I carry my camera body and two lenses, along with film, lens tissues, and such, in a Sima Sportpouch. This is an inflatable waterproof bag that looks much like a tiny air mattress with a zipper-lock top. I inflate it only partially (not really for floatation, but to cushion hard knocks) and keep it in our daypack. When I'm paddling, the daypack sits at my feet so that I can grab the camera almost instantly. Although this system is neither as watertight nor as protective as a hard case, it does provide adequate protection while still remaining a size that fits in the overflow daypack.

Photo opportunities abound

The market offers an array of accessory canoe bags designed to handle the odds and ends you may want to keep easily accessible. Some are bags that hang from thwarts. Although a great thing on day-long river trips where no portaging is encountered, they can be a nuisance on routes with frequent portages. Left on the canoe while portaging, they flop around and can even obstruct your vision. If you detach them at each portage, then you must find some way to attach them to another pack or carry them in your hand, which you should keep free for mashing mosquitoes.

Seat packs are a better alternative. These low-profile packs strap under your canoe seats. They are supported by the seat when the canoe is overturned while portaging, so they don't flop. Just be sure that you keep only lightweight items in them and that you balance the weight equally from bow to stern. I always cringe at adding more weight to the canoe though, and while I do find seat packs handy in some instances, the daypack seems to be the best compromise.

Fishing rods and your spare paddle should be lashed into the canoe, again with a nod toward balance, front to back.

Those whose canoes have slotted gunwales can easily attach these items with small webbing or velcro straps (the ones sold in ski shops for binding a pair of skis together work very well). If your canoe doesn't have slotted gunwales you might consider drilling holes for this purpose or you can lash the rods to the thwarts. The advantage of lashing rods to the gunwales, rather than the thwarts, is that they are nearer the outside edge of the canoe and won't interfere as much when packs are loaded or unloaded, and the rods gain some protection from breakage by being shielded by the gunwales. In either case, use straps or small rubber bungees rather than cords or tape. You'll want to get at the rods or spare paddle easily, and knots or tape will simply frustrate you.

All that should be left that isn't stuffed in a pack or lashed to the canoe are the paddles you are using and your life jackets. Again, the paddles can be jammed into the canoe, under thwarts or seats. Some folks permanently attach lengths of elastic cord under the bow thwart and yoke so that the paddles can be quickly and securely stowed for the portage. We generally just carry ours over the portage, except for the spare, which is always lashed into the canoe (with a quick-release hitch so that it can be freed instantly in a whitewater emergency).

Life jackets can be worn on portages, although they are hot. They can also simply be hung on the back of the pack, with the pack corners sticking through the arm holes. This works pretty well, but once in a while you'll get to the end of the portage and realize the PFD hasn't made it all the way across with you. Some folks zip the jacket around the canoe seat. Mostly, Mary Jo, who carries the food pack, just slings the lightweight PFDs on her arm or hangs them on the paddles she is carrying. It is important that everyone in your party know which pieces of equipment he or she is responsible for transporting across the portage. In that manner, nothing will be left behind because everyone assumed that someone else would be carrying it.

A wise oldtimer once gave me this simple tip:

Upon returning from your next canoe trip, make three piles when you unpack.

❏ In the first pile goes all those items you used frequently.

❏ In the second pile, place those things used only once in a great while.

❏ Finally, make a third heap of those things you never used at all.

Make notes, and on the next trip, take only those things in the first pile—with, of course, the exception of things like your first aid kit, which you hope you never use, but need just in case.

A party Mary Jo and I encountered between Koma and Polly Lakes gave us a compliment when they watched us hit the landing and take the portage. We pulled up, stepped into the water, and grabbed our packs. I helped Mary Jo get her packs on, handed her the paddles and PFDs and then slung on my own pack. I picked up the canoe and we were off.

"Wow," one observer exclaimed, "you guys are fast!"

I smiled and thanked him. Yes, we do move quickly, but not because we are in a hurry. With so many wonderful things to see and do in the canoe country, why labor intensively and unnecessarily on portages for hours?

By packing for the portage, counting ounces and pounds, and striving to have your gear organized so that it travels neatly and in one crossing, any of us can take all but the most arduous of portages in a single trip. If you can, the whole expanse of the canoe country awaits your exploration.

On Your Way, Finally

Both the greatest anticipation and the most apprehension concerning your canoe trip occur as you stand at the landing where your trip will begin. The car is parked. Packs are loaded into the canoe. Wind plays with your hair, sun dances on the waves. Ahead is the expanse of the first lake and beyond lies the wilderness, with all its glories and challenges. And you question, briefly, are we ready? Did we forget anything? Will we find our way? Then you shove off, dip your paddles into the gleaming waters, and leave the world you know fading behind. You are on your way, finally.

If you have planned well, packed smartly, and done your homework, all should go well.

That doesn't mean, however, that your learning experience is over or that there are not concerns and tests you'll need to face along the way. Perhaps the greatest gifts of any wilderness adventure are the difficulties and challenges, challenges so very different from those you meet in your everyday existence.

You may notice a few problems already as you begin to cross the first lake. Maybe your canoe handles poorly because it is bow heavy. Perhaps it seems to be listing slightly to one side. Obviously something is wrong, but what is it?

The wilderness awaits

❏ Are you ready?

❏ Did you forget anything?

❏ Will you find your way?

Loading the canoe

How you load your canoe is important not only to the manner in which it handles but also to your safety. When you refer to this weight distribution in a canoe, or any boat for that matter, it is called "trim." And it has nothing to do with decals or lights. A properly trimmed canoe (and there is more than one right way depending on conditions) will handle large seas better, track true in a tail wind, and turn more responsively when called upon. Under most conditions, you'll be able to get by with the weight distributed willy-nilly, but to really perfect your skills and minimize effort and danger, you should follow some basic tenets when placing cargo into your craft.

First things first. Canoes should be loaded in the water, not on land. I know, you've seen dozens of folks loading their canoe while it is grounded. You know what? They've all been doing it wrong. Your canoe is your most important piece of equipment. Put a hole in it back in the bush and pay for it with a long walk or spend time doing field repairs.

Second, when loading (or unloading) your canoe, pull it parallel to shore, not at a right angle. You don't park your car by driving it into a wall and you don't park your canoe by ramming it ashore. Rarely will you encounter a landing that won't allow you to bring your canoe to land in a parallel manner. Sometimes it does mean either the bow or stern passenger must exit first and then jockey the canoe into a proper position, but it almost always can be done. The biggest bane to a parallel landing are long underwater piles of rocks jutting into the lake, generally placed in the middle of what would have been a perfect spot to land parallel to shore.

Why pull the canoe in parallel to shore? Besides saving a lot of wear and tear on the hull, you'll find it is much easier to access your packs over the side of the canoe, allowing you to place them in just the position you want. Landing parallel to the shore is also much quieter because you won't have to

Step-by-step loading

❏ Load the canoe in the water

❏ Pull it parallel to shore

❏ One person steadies the canoe

❏ The other canoeist places packs

❏ Bow paddler enters canoe

❏ Bow paddler braces

❏ Stern paddler enters canoe

drag your loaded canoe over the granite to get it far enough ashore to get at your packs. Quiet is important. The sound of a canoe being dragged ashore travels a great distance; and while you may think you are alone in the wilderness, there are actually thousands of other campers around, hoping for a bit of peace and quiet. And finally, it is safer, since a canoe is never so tippy as it is when the bow is up on shore and one person remains astern.

Simply have one person steady the canoe from the side while the other places the packs in the bilge. When ready to depart, usually the bow person climbs aboard, nudging the bow out while entering, as the stern paddler steadies the canoe. Then the stern paddler climbs in while the bow person does a brace, which is accomplished by stretching the paddle and arm far out to one side with the blade flat on the water and applying downward pressure. This will ensure the canoe remains stable—almost as an outrigger does on those big Hawaiian canoes we've all seen on television. Try to always place your feet on the imaginary centerline of the canoe when stepping in and out. Brace your arms against the gunwales, dividing your weight evenly. Most canoes are tipped over in shallow water near shore, not in open water, and it usually occurs when someone is getting in or out improperly and their partner isn't steadying the canoe or bracing.

To land the canoe, reverse the process. It is always best to have the stern paddler exit first and enter last. All canoes are much broader under the bow seat than they are beneath the stern seat, which means the canoe will be a more a more stable platform with the bow person alone in the canoe than if just the stern paddler were aboard. This factor is greatly multiplied if the canoe is empty of cargo, as it might be on an evening excursion with all your gear in camp. Obviously, this is just the opposite of what most people do, for the majority of inexperienced paddlers leave or approach shore

Step-by-step unloading

- ❏ Unload the canoe in the water
- ❏ Pull it parallel to shore
- ❏ Bow paddler braces
- ❏ Stern paddler leaves canoe
- ❏ Bow paddler leaves canoe
- ❏ One person steadies the canoe
- ❏ Other canoeist places packs

at right angles. And just as obviously, unless the landing site is absolutely ideal, parallel landings and departures will require using the wet-foot technique.

The only time a parallel landing shouldn't be attempted is when you are coming to a shore that is being pounded by surf. Attempting a parallel landing in large seas is a sure way to swamp the canoe unless you are fast, strong, and lucky. Running the canoe straight in is the best technique, but in heavy seas you must work quickly to avoid damaging the hull or swamping the stern. Even then, the bow person should not jerk the canoe ashore but merely hold it in place while the stern paddler makes his way up to the bow and out. Then both should grab the canoe, each to a side and as near to the middle as possible, and lift the loaded canoe to shore. Some dragging will inevitably take place, but it is better than the alternatives of swamping in a parallel landing or not lifting, damaging the hull by dragging it fully loaded.

Portages can be busy thoroughfares

Portage etiquette

Move your equipment out of the way to make room for others

Whenever you are at a portage landing, practice portage etiquette. The simple rule is to move your equipment out of the way to allow for others who may come along. This is especially true if you double portage. We've often come to a portage strewn with canoes and packs in such a manner that it was nearly impossible for us to get ashore, and the owners of that equipment were somewhere down the trail hauling their first load across. It is aggravating, to say the least, to have to wait or to be forced to move someone else's gear. Prop fishing rods and other breakables against a tree or bush so that they aren't stepped on.

And when on the portage, be considerate of others you may encounter. Let people who are carrying canoes have the right of way. Last, the portage is often where people answer a call of nature. Fine. Just don't do it near the portage landing. It's a fact that on certain well-used routes, these landings become pretty unsanitary spots. Go down the trail a distance and then cut off into the woods. Bury all waste.

Load the canoe carefully for stability

When loading your gear into the canoe, take into account any weight difference between the bow and stern paddler and then place the packs accordingly so that all weight is evenly distributed fore and aft of the midpoint. If there must be any difference from front to rear, you are better off with a canoe that is slightly stern heavy than bow heavy. A bow-heavy canoe steers poorly.

Similarly, the load should be distributed evenly side to side. Often you won't notice the load isn't quite even until you are under way and you feel, more so than see, any listing. Usually nudging one pack over with your foot will be enough to regain balance.

You can also scoot your butt slightly to one side, unless your canoe has sculpted "tractor" seats, which limit a canoe's versatility. Many canoes with these seats have them located too far forward to be able to comfortably and effectively do a J-stroke, and they are often placed too low to cross your feet and ankles under, which is the best way to sit for a low center of gravity.

And of course, if you are paddling a tandem canoe by yourself, the best sitting position to do this from is the bow seat, reversed. With a traditional canoe seat that is not a great trick, but tractor seats are very uncomfortable to sit on when reversed. You can paddle solo from the stern seat only if you have placed enough duffel in the bow to trim the canoe. Paddling solo from the stern seat in an unloaded canoe is very risky.

Packs should be placed into the canoe so that they ride below the gunwale. This means they need to be laid flat. A seventeen-foot canoe can generally hold three #3 Duluth Packs this way. If you do need to carry more than that, one or more can be stood up in the canoe, but make sure they are widthwise (the flat side of the pack facing the bow or stern). If I have to stand packs up in the canoe, I often put them on edge. I do this because a Duluth Pack is a bit taller than it is wide, and when on edge, with the top and bottom each toward a gunwale, the pack will provide a profile six inches lower than if it were merely stood up. In any case, canoe packs shine compared to backpacks, because canoe packs adopt the contour of the canoe when lying flat and don't rise inordinately far above the gunwales even when standing.

Some folks get tense and stiff when in a canoe, no doubt because they are uncomfortable or scared. Unfortunately, that tense posture is more likely to tip you over than anything else, especially when it is combined with a sudden motion to one side. Relax. Let your weight sink to your behind. Open your legs so that your knees are at or below the gunwales, with your legs crossed at your ankles. Or you can stretch your legs out in front of you, both at once or one at a time with the other foot under the canoe seat. Relax your shoulders as well. If you adopt this posture, a lively canoe (paddler's euphemism for a tippy boat) will suddenly become much more stable.

Just to make sure nothing serious happens to you or your partner under any unfortunate circumstance, always wear a personal floatation device. Not doing so is just plain stupid. Modern PFDs are light in weight, unrestrictive, and comfortable to paddle in. After wearing one for awhile it becomes much like getting into the habit of wearing a seatbelt in your car: you feel naked without one.

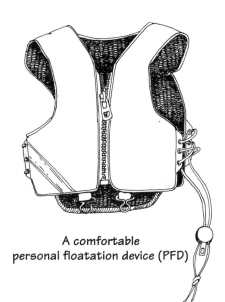

A comfortable personal floatation device (PFD)

When waves are high

Wind and waves can be a problem on the bigger lakes of the canoe country. Try to minimize the problem by getting underway at sunrise on days you must cross large expanses of water or by paddling at dusk. Unless a severe front is passing through, wind almost always comes and goes with the sun. Canoe country winds frequently arise from the west in the summer. You can sometimes plan a route along that shore so that you have a calm lee in which to paddle. Stay away from open expanses whenever possible. When paddling in a wind, the shortest distance between two points isn't a straight line. Hugging the shoreline, even if it is circuitous, will always be safer and easier, and will usually be faster.

Should you need to or choose to paddle in waves, you should strive to take them at a slightly quartering angle, paddling in the troughs and bracing, if necessary, at the crests. Good paddlers in well-designed canoes can ride out two-foot, even three-foot, seas.

Don't try it though if your canoe is of the racing-influenced low-bow, razor-edged, no-flare design. You'll be paddling a submarine if you do. A wilderness canoe should have just enough flare at the bow to assist it in rising with a wave, but not so much as to make the canoe slow. Watch the waves ahead of you as they approach. It seems as though every fourth or fifth wave will be bigger than average, so allow yourself the time to prepare.

Anticipate waves before venturing into them. In other words, if you are paddling in a sheltered area but can see the wind in the trees or spot whitecaps far out in the lake, evaluate your plans before rounding that point and leaving protection.

No one says you have to stick to a schedule. Being windbound is nothing to be ashamed of and can even be enjoyable as a change of pace. While we sometimes enjoy paddling in big seas just for the heck of it, if the distance to cross is so great that we would likely run out of energy before reaching calm water, we won't attempt it.

If we decide to take on a rough crossing, we often stop for a rest and a snack before venturing out into the waves. This does two things. It builds up some energy reserves you'll need for the crossing and it also gives you a chance to

In windy conditions hugging the shoreline will

❏ Always be safer

❏ Always be easier

❏ Usually be faster

Before venturing into rough water

❏ Stop

❏ Rest

❏ Have a snack

❏ Check your map

❏ Consider the risks
   very carefully

figure out the best approach (or to smarten up and wait it out). A glance at your map may show you an alternate route or a series of points and islands that will serve as both windbreaks and rest stops protected from the wind. Mistakes that result in a swamping generally don't happen when you're fresh; mostly the canoe will handle the situation if guided properly. But get pooped out, make a mental or physical error (even a misplaced stroke at an inopportune moment can be disastrous), and you could find yourself taking an unexpected swim. In the summer this may not be the most serious event you can imagine, but in the spring or fall, when water temperatures combined with chilly days and winds can lead to hypothermia, such errors can be fatal. Keep this in mind. A risk you might take in August could be foolhardy in May.

Know your abilities. I can tell you this much: you can handle bigger seas than you think, but you are definitely taking chances with your safety and equipment by doing so. The choice is yours. Make it wisely. And choose your partner carefully. Someone who gives out in a crossing or panics during a tense moment is likely to swamp the canoe and maybe kill you. Not funny stuff.

Running with the waves can be as exhilarating as paddling into them. Sometimes it is even more work since a canoe, like a sailboat, wants to turn bow upwind, especially if the canoe is bow heavy. This requires a lot of steering by the stern paddler, which can be tiring on a long reach. You will be traveling slower than the waves, so watch as they run down the length of canoe to see how much freeboard (distance from gunwale to wave top) you have. A couple of inches, at the midpoint of the canoe, is still quite safe. Some larger waves may occasionally slop into the canoe but unless you are paddling in big seas all day, not enough water will collect to be much of a problem. Use a large sponge to mop up this water, because you can work it into low spots between packs where a bailing bucket won't fit.

Lash your packs when waves are high

About the only time you need to lash your packs into your canoe is in big seas or in whitewater. Your waterproofed packs will add a lot of floatation to your canoe should you swamp far out in the lake. You also stand a good chance of losing your gear if you don't tie it in. Use nylon cord or rope and tie it to a thwart, crisscrossed over the packs and through their straps. For instance, start where the stern thwart joins the right gunwale, go diagonally across the canoe to the yoke at the left gunwale, wrap it, and then head diagonally to the bow thwart at the right gunwale, passing it through the straps on the packs as you go along. Now run the rope across the bow thwart to the left side and reverse the crisscrossing until you've reached the stern thwart/left gunwale location. Make sure the packs are tied as tightly to the bottom of the canoe as possible. You don't want them rising any farther from the floor than necessary. All knots should be quick-release types, such as half hitches, so that should you swamp, you can release them quickly once you get the canoe near shore. You don't want your fully loaded canoe pounding against rocks, and you certainly won't be able to get it out of the water (or the water out of it) if it is still carrying two hundred pounds of duffel.

In the event of such a swamping, stay with the canoe. A canoe full of lashed-in packs and water can even be steered and paddled. Doing so also allows you to get out of the water quickly. If your packs are not tied in, and float up and away, the canoe will not have enough buoyancy to support the two of you and will sink to below the surface, making it impossible to handle.

The best advice is to not put yourself into situations beyond your abilities. Second, in order to learn just what your abilities are, and what are the attributes of your canoe, practice dangerous maneuvers in shallow water on a hot

Safety tips

- ❑ Always wear a PFD
- ❑ Know your abilities and those of your partner
- ❑ Practice dangerous maneuvers in safe conditions
- ❑ Be extra careful in cold weather
- ❑ Lash your packs in high waves
- ❑ Stay with the canoe if it swamps
- ❑ Examine rapids before entering them

summer day, while wearing PFDs. Confidence can be built only through experience. The same is true for wisdom.

Whitewater in the canoe country generally falls into two categories: very easy and extremely dangerous. There isn't much in between. Remember the old paddler's axiom: no one ever drowned on a portage. When approaching whitewater, watch the shore or check your map for portages. If there is one, and you are doubtful of your skill, use the trail. There is a very big difference between running whitewater as a Saturday diversion near home, with dry clothes in your nearby car, and running whitewater far from help with the gear your life depends upon sitting in your canoe.

Many "rapids" marked on maps are small chutes of current between two lakes. Most of these are very easy to run even for the inexperienced. Legions of paddlers before you have stooped and groaned to move rocks and these rapids often resemble logging sluiceways through which it is easy to maneuver. However, until you know what is ahead, don't venture into even the easiest of rapids. If you can't see the end, or the route through, from your canoe, beach it and examine the route. Again, portages are a dead giveaway. If there's a portage, there's a reason.

Walking and lining the canoe

When the weather is warm, walking your loaded canoe up or down a simple rapids is an option. Be careful to keep a good grip and wear shoes to avoid injuring your feet. With the paddlers out, a canoe will float through many rock gardens that would otherwise require portaging.

Although it is not much used, the technique of lining a canoe upstream is effective and pretty easy to master. You can line downstream as well, but it is much riskier to your equipment. To line a canoe, attach a rope that is at least a quarter-inch in diameter to the bow as near to the waterline as possible. The rope for hanging your food packs will work just fine. Some canoes have a bow ring, otherwise known as a painter ring, affixed at the point where the bow reaches its fullest curve. This is an excellent location to which to tie ropes for both lining and towing. Ropes attached to the top of the deck or to grab handles can force the bow underwater, swamping the canoe.

A second rope, or the other end of the bow rope, is lashed to the stern thwart (except when lining downstream, when the aft rope should be tied to the stern, and the bow rope to the bow thwart). The canoe is nudged bow first away from shore into the current. With a firm grip on the rope(s), allow the bow to be forced slightly away from you. Think of the canoe now as a rudder. With the bow angling toward you, the current will force the canoe over to you. With the bow away from you, the canoe will work toward the far shore. While steering the canoe in such a manner, walk upstream. With a little practice you'll be able to effectively maneuver the canoe around obstructions.

Paddling skills

Your paddling skills will determine which conditions you can handle and how efficiently you can bring your canoe to shore. There are many different paddle strokes, and one could devote a whole book to describing the techniques. Indeed, venerable paddler Bill Mason did in his wonderful book *Path of the Paddle*, as well as in his video of the same name. Both are well worth studying.

For the most part, flat-water paddlers can get by with just a couple of simple strokes. Remember that bow and stern paddlers always operate on opposite sides of the canoe, except for rare coordinated special strokes. To begin with, you must understand the physics of paddling. The bow paddler, being nearest the midpoint of the canoe, has a tendency to overpower the stern paddler, unless the stern

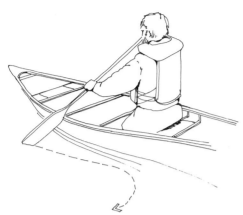

The J-stroke

The standard stroke for
stern paddlers

The stern sweep stroke

Used to turn the canoe in
the opposite direction

paddler is proportionally stronger. The bow paddler simply draws straight back on the stroke and for the majority of the time does not assist in steering. Think of the person in the bow as being the "motor" while the stern paddler is the "rudder." Because of this, many partners choose to put the strongest person in the bow. It is also the bow paddler's task to watch for underwater obstructions since visibility is unimpaired from this position. Polarized sunglasses really aid in this task and both paddlers should consider wearing them.

When the bow person is paddling on the left side, the canoe will have a tendency to veer to the right. The stern paddler corrects for this by employing a steering stroke while paddling on the right side. Beginners often steer by using the paddle as a rudder and this works just fine. But it has the serious drawback of slowing your progress since no power can be applied while ruddering. By far the most useful stroke for the stern paddler is the simple J-stroke, named for its shape. The J always opens away from the canoe. In other words, when viewed from above, the J-stroke looks like that letter when you're paddling on the left side, but is a mirror-image J when done to the right of the canoe.

To do the J-stroke, draw the paddle back with the blade at a right angle to the canoe. As it reaches the point near your hip, roll the lower hand forward until the knuckles face toward the canoe. Correspondingly, the thumb of the upper hand will point downward. Push the blade outward. The side of the paddle blade that was facing the stern (called the power face) should now face out, or away, from the hull of the canoe. The degree to which you push, or pry, away from the canoe will determine how much correction of direction is made. For most cruising, just a slight J motion is needed, and if the paddlers are matched well, it may only be needed every few strokes. You can also turn the canoe to the side on which the stern person is paddling by employing what is called a "heavy J" by applying more strength and greater prying for a longer duration. If the bow person also applies a heavy J on the opposite side of the canoe, you can turn your craft quickly.

To turn the canoe in the opposite direction, without the paddlers switching sides, the stern paddler employs the "stern sweep" stroke. With the bow person paddling straight back on the left side of the canoe, the stern paddler pulls the paddle back in a sweep that brings the power face toward the hull at the end of the stroke. Unless you have a canoe with the seat placed too far forward of the stern, the stroke could actually end up beyond the end of the canoe. A shallow sweep is often used as a course correction stroke, just like a shallow J-stroke, but to the opposite direction. A wide sweep, especially combined with a little help from the bow paddler (who reaches out diagonally and draws the power face toward his or her body), will turn a canoe quickly away from the stern paddler's side.

Initially, you should also learn a couple of other simple paddle techniques. Earlier I mentioned the brace technique. This is done to stabilize the canoe, for instance, when someone is getting in or out. This technique involves a lot of trust that water will indeed support you. You must lean far out over the water, your hands still in the paddling position (one on the hand grip, one near the throat where the shaft joins the blade) and push down on the power face. The effect, as stated earlier, is of an outrigger.

Bringing the canoe parallel to shore requires some maneuvering strokes that are more commonly associated with whitewater, which is probably why so many otherwise experienced flatwater paddlers couldn't "parallel park" their canoe if their life depended upon it.

The simplest way to move your canoe sideways, as you'll need to do at a landing, is to use the draw stroke. One paddler, or both paddlers depending on the situation, reaches toward shore straight out from his or her hip and pulls the paddle back to the canoe, with the shaft nearly straight up

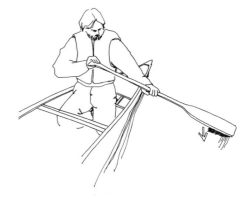

The brace technique

Stabilizes the canoe like an outrigger

The draw stroke

Pulls the canoe sideways for landing

115

and down and the blade facing the hull. When the paddle nears the canoe, pull it from the water, reach out and repeat the process as many times as necessary to get to where you need to go. In shallow water, much of the stroke might need to be done with just the tip of the blade. If done on just one end of the canoe, only that end is brought toward shore. To move both ends simultaneously, both paddlers should do the stroke. This technique, by the way, can also be done in a moving canoe or in whitewater to quickly pull the canoe away from an obstruction.

Another sideslipping maneuver is called the pry stroke. It is in essence the exact opposite of the draw stroke. With the blade parallel to the hull, the paddler pushes away from the canoe. It is called the pry stroke because most often it is done by using the gunwale of the canoe as a fulcrum and the paddle as a lever, which makes it very powerful.

You can combine these two techniques to move a canoe laterally or to pivot it. For instance, if the stern paddler is operating on the right and does a draw stroke, while the bow paddler does a pry stroke on the left, the canoe will scoot to the right. If you wish to pivot the canoe, try having each paddler do a draw stroke, but on opposite sides of the canoe. Or each do a pry stroke, again on opposite sides. You can turn a canoe on a dime this way.

For real delicacy and refinement in moving a canoe sideways to or away from shore, eventually you should learn the sculling stroke. This is done by drawing the paddle toward you (reaching out from the canoe as in the draw

The pry stroke

Pushes the canoe sideways

The sculling stroke

Moves the canoe sideways powerfully and quietly

stroke) but with the blade at a slight angle to the canoe. As you pull back, the paddle will travel diagonally to the side. When it has gone a foot or so, reverse the angle, pull toward the canoe and allow the paddle to travel a foot in the opposite direction. You are inscribing in the water a sort of sideways figure eight. Unlike the draw stroke, where the paddle leaves the water between strokes, the sculling stroke is done completely underwater. It is exceedingly powerful and very quiet and is useful not only to bring the canoe to shore but to quietly position the canoe while photographing wildlife or fishing. With practice, with your hand very near the top of the blade you can even do it one-handed.

Many other canoe strokes exist that will allow you to gracefully yet forcefully make your canoe dance to the tune you wish to play. These will come with experience and practice. The simple strokes described here, however, will give you all the techniques you'll need to maneuver a canoe as if you've been doing it all your life.

A stroke that is currently in fashion amongst racers is called the "hut" stroke. Both paddlers stroke strongly straight back and as the canoe starts to veer from a straight line (since no steering is employed), the stern paddler calls "hut" and both switch paddling sides. Effective for fast, straight-ahead paddling, it is nonetheless an arhythmic stroke that takes a lot of the smoothness out of a wilderness tour.

You can adopt, however, the best of the "hut" technique and apply it to the straight-ahead steering strokes outlined above, namely the J-stroke and sweep stroke. To do so, paddlers should paddle on opposite sides. But paddling all day each to one side is not only tiring but inefficient. Switching sides allows you to rest one set of muscles while using another. While "hut" strokers may switch on every five or six strokes, most wilderness canoeists would be better off finding a rhythm more suited to them. After trying a number of strokes per side from five to forty, Mary Jo and I found that switching sides every twenty strokes works very

The "hut" stroke

Used by racers for fast, straight-ahead paddling

117

well for us. We paddle hard and fast for twenty strokes, during which time I throw in a few J-strokes or sweep strokes to maintain a straight line. At twenty strokes I call aloud "hut" and we switch. We've been known to keep this up for twenty miles.

It really doesn't make any difference who calls "hut" as long as one person is in charge. Some leave it up to the bow person, who simply switches on the predetermined number while the stern paddler watches for the switch and reacts. Whatever the case, if you leave it to the guess-and-by-golly technique, you'll be veering all over the place.

Watch good paddlers as they go by. Invariably you'll see them paddling in unison with crisp, clean side-switches. Such technique is the mark of an experienced team or of two experienced paddlers who, though they may never have occupied a canoe together before, knew enough to quickly decide upon a rhythm.

Finding your way through the wilderness

Now that you can cruise along nicely, you have to be able to find your way. Excellent maps for both the Boundary Waters Canoe Area Wilderness and Quetico exist, and only a fool would venture out without a good map and a compass. Very little of your navigation, however, will be done with classic map and compass techniques such as triangulation and the taking of bearings. These methods, though wise wilderness skills to master, are needed primarily when traveling cross-country or across wide expanses of water; in both cases, your destination will be out of sight. Maintaining a compass bearing then will be critical.

You, however, won't be rambling long distances through the tangled canoe country forest. Nor will you be on lakes so large that pinpoint navigation will be critical. Mostly you will use your compass and map to point you toward the right direction, and you'll take most of your navigation cues from

Study your map carefully— notice and remember

❏ Points
❏ Bays
❏ Islands
❏ River mouths
❏ Campsites

matching islands, points, and campsites on the map to the ones you see in front of you.

Always orient your map to the direction you're traveling. By this I mean lay the map in front of you on a pack and, if you are traveling north, have the north end of the map furthest away from you. Since even relatively small lakes can have a lot of points, bays, and islands that may confuse you, study the map before setting out. Remember key features such as river mouths, campsites, and the like. As you paddle north, keep comparing the visible features to the map features. Over there is the river that corresponds to this one on the map. Diagonally from you you can see the campsite on a point that is also marked on the map. Here's that funny-looking, horseshoe-shaped island. And so on.

If in doubt, paddle near shore. If the portage you seek is on the west side of the lake, travel along that shoreline to ensure you don't bypass it. The vast majority of campsites and portage trails in the canoe country are visible from quite a distance away because of the soil erosion. Another visible clue is a lack of undergrowth.

If you've reached an area where a portage is supposed to be, but from out in the lake you are still having a hard time discerning exactly where it is, take a look at the surrounding topography. Almost always, portages occur in the lowest location, which also often signifies the presence of a creek, which portages frequently follow. Since time unfathomable, people have been utilizing these trails, as have wildlife, none of which like to climb over hills if a flatter route exists. So look for low areas.

Also consider that it would be a foolish canoeist that would carry a canoe an inch farther than necessary. Therefore, portages generally begin at the deepest recess of a bay, or even part way up a creek, to shorten the distance. Only when cliffs or steep hills intervene is this rule broken.

Take frequent compass readings, especially on overcast days. On winding lakes such as Kawnipi or Crooked, it is

Where is that portage?

❏ In a clearing

❏ In a low area

❏ In the deepest recess of a bay

❏ Partway up a creek

119

quite possible to find yourself paddling west down a blind bay when you thought you were heading north in the main channel, all because you lost count of points or islands and hadn't been checking your compass.

Wandering around may sometimes lead to serendipitous discoveries of seldom-used campsites or wildlife, but it can also slow your progress greatly.

Looking for the perfect campsite

Paddling into such back bays and along shorelines, away from that imaginary straight line between the two portages, can be a wise thing to do.

When Mary Jo and I served as wilderness rangers, we noticed that the campsites nearest the most direct-line route were always occupied, consequently dirty, and seldom as pretty as those just a mile or so away, tucked off the main travel route, which hadn't suffered overuse and were always more pleasant. The fishing was better too. Since that time we have always sought out those back-bay sites and reaped the benefits of solitude and cleanliness. In the Quetico, where there are no designated campsites, we've discovered pristine camping spots we were quite certain hadn't been occupied in years, perhaps decades. These are real treasures.

By the way, just recently mapmakers have begun marking Quetico campsites on the maps, something I consider a disservice to the resource. You must understand that the two wildernesses operate in fundamentally different manners regarding people management.

On the U.S. side, the Forest Service handles the heavier traffic by insisting everyone camp in a designated site so that fires and sanitation can be controlled with permanent fire grates and latrines.

Quetico spreads out its lighter use, and the sometimes unhealthy sanitary practices of campers, by letting people camp where they wish. This has the effect, when sites aren't

A straight line is not necessarily the best way to travel through the wilderness

too frequently used, of allowing nature to do much of the maintenance. But when maps direct people via red dots to specific sites in the Quetico, sites that have no latrines to handle the increased use, the system fails. Either all sites should be mapped, or none.

Preparing to portage

Now that you've managed to master a few paddle strokes and find your way across the lake, and even learned how to properly land your canoe at the portage, only the portage remains.

We've learned how you should pack for the portage; how fishing rods, spare paddles, and other loose items should either be lashed in or otherwise carried; and how everyone should be assigned specific packs and items to make sure everything gets to the other end of the trail without losses. Only one thing remains: picking up and carrying the load.

Getting into your pack's straps is easier if someone gives you a hand. If you have to do it yourself, however, try this. Grab the pack by the ears. If you are right-handed, bend your left knee and place the pack on it, straps facing you. Dip your right shoulder, sneak the right arm through the strap to your left, and slide it up to your shoulder. Your left hand coordinates the movement by helping to lift the pack. With the pack now on your back, hunch over so that the pack's weight is fully on the flat of your back and not the shoulder straps, and snake your left arm through the remaining shoulder strap. Sounds awkward, but it really isn't.

Although you may be tempted to try it, and it might seem logical, trying to get a canoe across the portage with two people carrying it is really very inefficient. The one-person carry evolved because in all but the rarest of circumstances, it is by far the best way to portage a canoe. In fact, one could say that it was portability that was the motivation in the canoe's development.

Lifting and carrying the canoe

Carrying the canoe is relatively easy with the use of a good padded portage yoke. Some traditionalists still lash their paddles into the canoe at each portage and use the flat of the blades as shoulder rests. Though this works pretty well, it is really a practice more common to the East, where portages are much more infrequent. In the Quetico and BWCAW, with the frequent carries you'll encounter, the portage yoke, which replaces the center thwart, is an investment you'll not want to do without.

No, it's not the carrying that most folks find difficult; it is getting the canoe up onto the shoulders that many find so cumbersome. Actually, the task is quite simple if the canoe is of a reasonable weight, no matter what your size or strength. Flipping a canoe to your shoulders is much more a matter of technique than it is strength. By all means, practice this in your backyard before departing. Dropping the canoe on grass is much better than dropping it on granite. If you are renting a canoe, have the outfitter teach you how to lift and flip the canoe before you depart.

Describing this isn't easy. Remember that as I describe each step, they are not really separate but flow into each other in one fluid motion. If you stop somewhere along the line you'll probably not succeed. Momentum is the name of the game. Instructions are for right-handed people. Southpaws need merely reverse them (and stand on the other side of the canoe).

With the canoe upright and on the ground (or in the water), stand amidships, on the left side of the hull, bow to your left. You should be facing the yoke, which opens toward the bow. With both hands grab the gunwale nearest you, about one foot on each side of the yoke, and pull the canoe up so that it slides onto your thighs. The open hull is now facing away from you, the canoe bottom is resting on your thighs.

The rest of the maneuver must be done in one continuous motion. Keeping your left hand on the gunwale a foot or so toward the bow from the yoke, move your right hand to the center of the yoke. Begin to lift and pull the canoe up further onto your hips. About halfway, move your left hand from its position on the near gunwale to the far gunwale. Continue rolling the canoe up. The open hull is now more or less beginning to face you. Quickly move your right hand (which was on the yoke) to the near gunwale, a foot behind the yoke. Some folks actually put this hand under the hull so that the gunwale would be cradled at the elbow joint. With a pelvic thrust, drive the canoe out and up with a coordinating roll with the arms (you are now lifting with the right arm, holding up and pulling across your body with the left); roll the canoe up to your shoulders. Duck your head forward so that you can get the yoke past it without knocking your hat (or head) off. Center the pads on your shoulders. It's up!

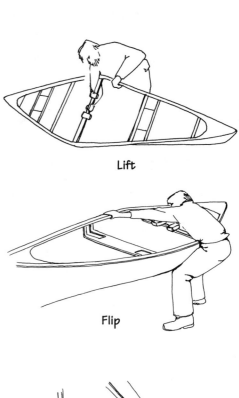

Lift

Flip

I know it sounds confusing. But mastering this technique is not difficult once you figure out what the heck I'm talking about. Lowering the canoe is just a reversal of the described technique, only you'll have gravity on your side this time. I prefer to pick the canoe up from the water. It is less damaging to the hull and—this is important—a foot nearer your shoulders since it is floating. Be sure that you have good footing before attempting to lift the canoe or you could suffer a fall.

If you are unable to master this technique, there is another method. It does involve some abuse to the canoe, however. Stand at the stern and roll the canoe upside down. Lift the stern above your head and with arms outstretched, alternately bounce your hands down each gunwale until you reach the yoke. Step beneath it and then lift up the bow. If you have a partner, have him or her hold one end up while

Carry

123

you slide beneath the yoke. Be aware that eventually you're going to wear down the deck plate of your canoe, especially if you use this technique much in the granite-boned canoe country.

While carrying a canoe, reach both hands forward and grab the gunwales. This will allow you to pull, or push, the bow up or down. When going downhill, you'll need to pull the bow down somewhat so that you don't smash the stern deck on the ground behind you. The opposite is done going uphill. As in a semitrailer truck, you need to make wide turns with a canoe to avoid banging into trees. If you didn't discover it before, you'll know by now if your canoe is well balanced. Improper yoke placement, as well as tied-in fishing rods or spare paddles, can make the canoe heavier on one end. It is very tiring on a long portage to have to hold up, or pull down, one end of the canoe. You can make temporary adjustments to balance by wedging a life jacket into one end or the other (or zip it around a seat) to compensate.

Try to lower your canoe at the end of the portage either entirely over the water or at least with the bow extending from shore. Many canoes are damaged at the end of the carry, when a tired voyageur lets the canoe slip while lowering it to the ground. If you drop it over water, no damage can occur.

In the BWCAW there are still a few of the old canoe rests around (horizontal poles lashed between trees) on which you can rest the bow of the canoe to spell yourself. Most have deteriorated and are not being replaced, and rightfully so. Such artifices have no place in a wilderness. Rarely are there branches of convenient size and height to serve as a canoe rest. If you get pooped, put the canoe down or wedge the bow between two trees along the trail. (Of course, such procedure has always been the norm in the Quetico, where canoe rests were never constructed.)

You can spell each other as well if you stay near your compadre. If the person carrying the canoe gets tired, the partner sheds the packs, steps beneath the bow of the canoe, and with the stern resting on the ground, relieves the canoe portager of the burden. Then they reverse roles, and continue down the trail.

Portaging is largely a psychological battle, not a physical one. I've seen folks drop their load within yards of the unseen end of a portage, only because they figured that the trail must be endless. Know how long your portage is before beginning. A rod is sixteen feet. A mile is 5,280 feet. Since you can walk a mile in twenty minutes, even when carrying a canoe (unless the portage is inordinately steep or muddy), glance at your watch before beginning. Most portages in the canoe country will take you ten minutes or less, which sounds a lot less frightening than 120 rods. I'm sure you can carry a canoe for five to ten minutes at a crack; and once you've built up your portage muscles, mile portages can be taken, even when carrying both a canoe and a pack, without a rest stop.

Once you learn to trim a canoe, to perfect your paddle strokes, to master the map, and to confidently pick up and portage your canoe, your canoeing adventure will be not only easier but much more fun. Skills are confidence builders. Wilderness tests your skills. When you've reached the level where you know that you can take what the wilderness is dishing up, or that you should defer to nature, you will find yourself much more comfortable in the rugged environs of the Quetico-Superior canoe country.

Most portages will take less than ten minutes—that's not too tough

The Movable Home

A gentle breeze slips softly through pines, sighing. Across the lake the sun settles in for the night, its lowering light a ruddy orange, the sky above it purple. The campfire crackles, snapping sparks toward the first stars. Wood smoke smells fine, the lapping little waves sound better. You settle back with feet to the fire and eyes on the sunset, slightly stiff back and sore shoulders enjoying their rest. Your thoughts turn to the day's adventures, the many tasks, the snug camp you've just secured for the night. You feel as though you've just walked into your own home after a long absence. Yes, home. Your home in the woods.

For me one of the greatest charms of wilderness travel is the complete sense of independence, the knowledge that all you need to move freely through the world is in your head or stashed in the pack. That gear pack, that ornery pack that seemed so miserably heavy on the trail, really represents freedom. In it is your movable home, in it are all the trappings you need to secure a spot to sleep, to cook, to eat. When you think of it, despite the weight of the pack, it is really quite amazing that you have been able to pare down your life so that it fits in one pack. And that is a lesson that you should be taking home with you.

Your campsite is your reward at the end of the day. Any who have traveled this canoe country know that there are

A crackling campfire, the smell of woodsmoke, a crimson sunset over a deep blue lake—you are at home in the wilderness

127

A *choice* campsite has

❏ A flat, high tent site

❏ Access to a breeze

❏ A shelf-rock landing

❏ Seasoned firewood

❏ A place to hang the food pack

❏ As much privacy as you want

campsites, and then there are CAMPSITES. Upper-case campsites have special qualities, such as a view of the sunset or sunrise or, luckiest of all, of both. They are generally endowed with tent sites that are both flat and high, flat for comfort and high to catch the wind and to keep from turning into puddles in a rainstorm. The choicest campsites haven't been so worn down that the interior of the site is nothing more than bare dirt and wood chips. The choicest campsites also have wonderful shelf rock landings that make getting in and out of the canoe a pleasure, not a chore. And the best campsites have what the old time woodsmen called good "wood chance," referring to the availability of seasoned firewood.

Perhaps it is too much to expect all those things in one site, but they do exist and are always a pleasure to find. Even sites that at first glance seem to offer little often turn out to be memorable spots for one or more reasons. Despite wind and weather, bugs and bears, I've never met a campsite I didn't like.

There is much more to consider, however, when looking for a campsite, than the view. Your safety and enjoyment will be much influenced by not only what type of site you choose but how you set up your camp and how you care for that site.

Unfortunately, much of what I'm about to say may not apply sometimes if you are camping in the BWCAW. After all, since you are required to camp in a designated site (remember, a BWCAW site must have both a permanent fire grate and a wilderness box latrine), you may not have the luxury of choice in some situations. For instance, if your destination is Manyflies Lake, and there is but one designated campsite on it, well, you don't have much choice. Or if Manyflies Lake has three sites, but two are already occupied, the story is the same. It pays, when traveling in the BWCAW, to start looking for a campsite in the early afternoon, especially if you are near entry points or on main travel routes or are heading into an area where campsites are few and far between.

If you are a competent voyageur and the weather permits, you can forego the just-stated advice, IF you are willing to push on no matter the time or distance it takes to find an unoccupied site. Through experience Mary Jo and I have found that an unoccupied site is rarely more than another portage or another few miles of water travel away. But making the decision to keep traveling depends on your abilities: if you or your partners are already growing weary, stop at the first available site.

Camping illegally simply isn't an option unless the situation is life threatening (such as in a lightning storm). If you reach your destination only to find there is no campsite, calm yourself, take a break, and examine the alternatives. A quick glance at your map will show you where the next site is located. Chances are another thirty to sixty minutes of travel will get you there.

If you are tired, take a long break and have a hearty snack. With your energy restored, the additional miles will fall easily. Part of the challenge you accepted upon entering the wilderness is to sometimes push yourself beyond what you normally would attempt. You also accepted the challenge to care wisely for the wilderness, and that means adhering to the regulations. Increase your odds of finding an unoccupied site by choosing a lake that is off the main travel route. Even in the BWCAW there are sites that are rarely used. Just the effort of seeking a remote bay on an otherwise busy lake is often enough to ensure the campsite will be waiting for you.

In the Quetico such worries go right out the window. You can camp wherever you wish as long as you don't go hacking out a bunch of live vegetation to do so. Although the majority of campsites aren't marked on maps of the Quetico, it isn't hard to imagine where they might be just by

If the BWCAW campsite you want is occupied

❑ Stop and take a break
❑ Have a snack or a meal
❑ Check your map for nearby sites
❑ Don't camp illegally

If the Quetico location you want is occupied

❑ Stop and take a break
❑ Check your map for likely sites—points or islands
❑ Paddle on till you find a pleasant site

looking at a map of the lake. Points and islands are always good spots to check out. It is the rare lake that won't have a decent place to spend the night. And although Quetico sites aren't "designated," they have been used before and are visible from the water. Any outcrop of shelf rock flowing down to the water's edge is a good place to check out. We often choose to paddle into the late afternoon, or even early evening, when in the Quetico. The temperature moderates then and the wind generally dies. This far north it is light until nine or ten o'clock, so even arriving at a site during the dinner hour allows for plenty of time to make camp.

But even in the Quetico we try to stay away from campsites that look too well used, for a very simple reason: sanitation. Upon arriving in a Quetico site that looks fairly well used, we split up and take a short walk around the perimeter of the camp. If there are unburied piles of human waste and heaps of toilet paper, we move on, unless traveling further isn't an option. Then we bury the waste and make the best of it. Quetico officials freely admit that sanitation is the biggest problem they face regarding visitor management.

Suppose you have a choice, whether in the BWCAW or Quetico, of campsites. What, besides the luxuries of view and smooth landings, makes a good site? Here are our preferences.

Before we even begin to check out sites, we study the map. If the sites are marked on it, we consider things such as how far the site is from its nearest neighbor and how close it may be to the portage. While we're not antisocial, we'd just as soon not be camped near others or passing traffic. Everyone benefits from a sense of solitude.

Then we focus on camp qualities we feel are important. We like places that are exposed to the wind, since that helps keep the mosquitoes at bay. Once we've spotted one (these sites are usually on points or islands), we land and look for cleanliness and for good tent sites (and in the BWCAW, both a fire grate and latrine). A good tent site is one that is flat (they're never perfect, of course), and isn't below towering white or red pines (deadly in lightning storms), nor below snags (standing dead trees) that may topple in a wind. If the site is otherwise suitable, except for a snag, we'll see if we can push it over, eliminating the risk (although this in itself is risky, so be careful). We prefer tent sites that are on a high elevation, rather than at water level, since water flows downhill, and we prefer not to sleep in puddles.

The next requirement on our list is a good place to hang the food pack. If an obvious branch is visible on a big pine, I check the bark for claw marks as an indication of bear troubles. Litter back in the woods is sometimes an indication of bears. It may mean some slobs camped in that spot, but it often means that a bear dined on someone's freeze-dried Szechuan shrimp.

Finally, if in the Quetico, we look for a good spot well away from the water to dig a shallow pit latrine. Small islands rarely afford an adequate site. Latrines should be located at least one hundred feet from the water to avoid polluting the lake.

Of minor concern is the wood chance. It is a blessing, of course, to have good wood readily available, but even if the site is picked over (if you've traveled to an out-of-the-way spot like we do, picked-over sites are rare), it is a simple matter to get in the canoe and paddle down the shore a distance. There is no shortage of firewood in the canoe country, just in some campsites.

A lot of folks choose islands for campsites, not because they offer a view or relief from mosquitoes, but because they think they won't have to hang their food pack. WRONG. Bears swim very well, thank you. We've been raided on island campsites and have witnessed, on more than one occasion, bears swimming far out into large lakes, obviously intent on a little raid. The best defense against losing your food to bears is to adequately hang your packs. We'll cover that in detail in "Bugs, Bears and Other Travel Travails."

Bears can swim

131

Fires and fire safety

A campfire is part of the charm of a canoe trip. Those of you whose camping experience stems from primarily alpine backpacking may question the ethics of a campfire. You'd be correct to wonder about the propriety of fires if this were an alpine setting, where soils are damaged easily and firewood is scarce. The story is different in the canoe country, where there is no shortage of firewood. Downed dead trees are abundant. Most campfires are located on mineral soil or on the ever-present granite, and so scarring is kept to a minimum. Just keep in mind that campfires, though cheery, can also devastate the forest if they are allowed to escape the confines of the fireplace.

The U.S. Forest Service has installed permanent steel fire grates at all BWCAW campsites. These grates are located on safe soil or rock and away from overhanging branches that may catch fire. Your fire MUST be built in the grate. Not near it, not on top of it, but in it. And it must be extinguished every time you leave camp, even if it is just to go fishing. Campsites and entire forests have been burned up by careless campers who have left an unattended fire. If protecting your gear isn't motive enough for dousing the fire, consider that it is also illegal to leave your fire unattended. A fine might dampen your trip if you don't do the same to the fire.

Although there aren't fire grates in the Quetico, it is a rare campsite that doesn't have a well-used rock fire ring. You are required by Ontario law to locate your campfire in a safe place—on mineral soil or rock and away from trees. If in doubt, build your fire on rock, near the water's edge. Most fire rings are located in pretty safe locations. Don't build a new one unless you believe the fire ring isn't in a safe location. Nothing will make a campsite ugly more quickly than a plethora of blackened fire pits. Be aware that a few

Fire grate

Quetico sites have two fire pits, one near the water and another near the rear of the camp in a sheltered location. These second fire locations are generally for winter or spring use, when protection from cold winds and precipitation is needed. Don't build fires in them during the summer—they are unsafe during dry conditions.

Camping in the Quetico means hauling two pieces of equipment you wouldn't need in the BWCAW: a fire grate and a garden trowel. A small backpacker's fire grate, or a wire shelf from an old refrigerator, is needed if you plan on cooking on wood. We wrap our grate in an old pillow case to avoid blackening the inside of the pack in which it is carried. The garden trowel, a digging tool, is used to dig a small pit for your latrine. Locate a spot well away from the lake or river and dig a shallow hole (6–8 inches deep), carefully cutting away the sod and saving it. If you want a little added comfort, lash a pole of dead wood between two trees above the hole to provide a place to sit. As you use the latrine, sprinkle a little of the dirt removed from the hole over the toilet paper to keep it from blowing around. When you leave for good, fill in the hole, remove the pole and place the piece of sod back on top. If this is done correctly, no one will know where your latrine was.

Selecting and gathering firewood

Speaking of cooking on wood, many camping books go to great lengths to describe the types of wood, and comparative BTUs, used in fire building. I recommend one type of wood: dead and dry. Though many tree species inhabit the Quetico-Superior wilderness, the most common dead, dry woods are spruce and fir. Birch that is dead is usually rotten, since the bark retains moisture. Cedar is sometimes available and works well. Aspen burns readily if not punk.

The important thing to remember about gathering firewood is to select only trees that have fallen down and are

Ideal firewood is

❑ dead

❑ down

❑ dry

thoroughly dry. Standing dead trees should be left where they are as they provide habitat for many creatures. To determine if wood is truly dry, break a twig. If it snaps, you're all set. If you must twist it off, it will give you some trouble. Spruce, pine, and fir with green needles still attached will burn poorly.

By far the best size of wood for cooking is the easily gathered small-to-medium branches. Mostly thumb- to wrist-size, they are quick to gather, can be broken to length (just lean them against a log or stump and stomp on them), and are the best size for cooking. Cooking means flame regulation. Small pieces of wood allow you to add just the amount of fuel you need and work much better than large chunks. You want a small, hot fire. Big fires are hard to work near, because the heat drives the cook away.

We rarely take an ax with us these days. The only real use for an ax is to get at dry wood inside a log by splitting. Although that's an important task when cooking solely on wood during wet weather, you can cook more quickly on a lightweight backpacking stove. We routinely cook on wood but relegate cooking to the stove in inclement weather. A small folding saw can be useful too, but I'd guess that in the last few years we have been able to gather most of the wood we've needed without either the ax or the saw.

To build a fire

Despite a lot of old tales, there is no trick to building a fire if you have dry tinder and wood. Conifer needles, twists of dry grass, or birch bark (taken only from downed trees, or better yet, from the many pieces littering the forest floor, shed from standing trees) work well as tinder. Birch bark, even when wet, easily catches fire. Get a good pile of tinder together and then build a tepee of sorts over it with pencil-diameter dry sticks. Always have the next size firewood (thumb diameter) broken to length and stacked near at hand. Once the tepee is built,

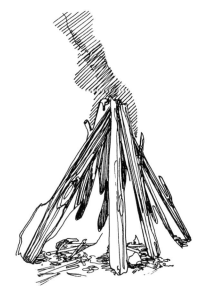

Tepee fire

strike a match to it; when it is completely engulfed, start adding the slightly bigger pieces of wood. Try to prop these upright as well. A fire needs oxygen and the tepee method, or the alternative, a sort of pyramid built log-cabin style, meets the need. Don't wait too long before adding more wood, but also don't add so much so early that you snuff the flames. Practice makes perfect.

If you gather firewood during dry weather and store it beneath the canoe or a tarp whenever you are away from camp, or at night, you won't need to worry about hacking away with an ax to get dry wood. The only time we revert to carrying an ax is in the early spring or late autumn, when a fire is not just a luxury but a means of keeping warm and drying clothing. Indeed, a fire at that time of the year may be a lifesaver should you swamp your canoe. Make sure your ax is extremely sharp. Believe it or not, a sharp ax is much safer than a dull one, which requires Herculean effort to split wood and leads to misplaced blows that generally end up in someone's leg. Sharp axes split dry wood easily.

To prepare it for the ax, cut wood to foot-long lengths with your folding saw. Wood doesn't need a large diameter to be dry inside. Four- to six-inch diameter is best. Always split wood on a chopping block or log. Otherwise you will dull the ax quickly when you strike stones. Stand the chunk up, leaning it slightly away from you against a log. With a moderate blow, start the ax into the top of the log. The blade should wedge into the wood. Finish splitting the wood by sending the ax and wood down with a blow to the top of the chopping log. It should split easily. Repeat until you have quartered the chunk. For kindling, keep splitting until you have fine splints.

Campsites get a severely "used" look if firewood is gathered within the site. Resist cutting dead limbs from campsite trees. If you can't find enough good firewood next to camp, make a foray down the lake and load up your canoe with the abundant dead wood you'll find. When doing this, don't

Firewood stacked under tarp

saw off exposed dead trees leaning over the water. They provide important fish sanctuary and shade.

No-trace camping benefits everyone

As the number of people who wish to visit the wilderness increases, the practice of "no-trace" camping becomes more and more important. Though you may see very few people on your trip, some two hundred thousand people will visit the combined Quetico-BWCAW region each year, most of those on the U.S. side. Because of the number of visitors, resource damage is cumulative. You may not think that your actions are important, but multiply a destructive deed by the number of visitors and you can see how quickly the resource can be marred. Leaving no trace of your passing not only makes the next visitor's trip more pleasant but should be a matter of pride among your crew. It is also your responsibility to make suggestions to those in your party who are not practicing good no-trace techniques.

Some of the worst offenders are people who have been camping for years. Assuming that their experience equals good technique, many continue to use damaging outmoded camping methods. Remember, a few decades ago the standard practice among campers in this region was to bury trash behind the camp or weight it with rocks and sink it in the lakes! Times have changed, but not all campers have changed their methods. For instance, many folks still do washing in the lakes. Even some outfitters continue to distribute bars of Ivory soap or biodegradable detergents, implying that such products don't harm the environment. Well, I don't know about you, but I don't take my drinking water from the bathtub. And the critters that live in the lakes and stream deserve more consideration than to use their home as a sink.

Do your dishes and bathing away from the lakes and streams. Biodegradable or not, all soap pollutes. Heat your dishwater in the largest pot of your cook kit, and haul your dirty dishes to an area behind your camp. Wash and rinse your dishes there, where the soil microbes can safely break down the soap. Bathing should also be done away from the lake, using a solar shower or pots filled with water. What we often do is go for a swim and then walk back up into the forest to lather up. While I'm doing this, Mary Jo brings a few pots of rinse water up to me. When I've eliminated as much soap from my skin and hair as possible, I go for another swim and then handle the rinse water for Mary Jo.

Laundry can be simply and efficiently done in a heavy duty plastic bag, which gets the clothing cleaner than washing in the lake and eliminates water pollution. The simple technique is given in "Good Gear = Good Trip."

Sometimes you'll end up with food leftovers. If you plan your menu carefully, this should rarely happen; but should it occur, never dump food in the water or in the woods near camp. No one wants to look at your two-day-old macaroni where they swim or take drinking water and no, the minnows won't eat it (at least not fast enough to avoid an unsightly mess for the next campers). Food dumped behind camp attracts insects and bears. To get rid of excess food, build a hot, hot fire and burn it in small quantities.

Never dispose of foods in the latrine. Bears have no qualms about smashing a latrine to get at those goodies.

All nonburnable trash should be packed out. No foodstuffs in nonreusable or nonburnable cans or bottles are allowed in the canoe country. We burn as much as we can along the way, even plastics. (One fellow chastised me, during a seminar I was giving, about this practice because he felt it pollutes the air. Yes, it does. Had I hauled the plastic home, it would have ended up in a landfill or been burned in the local incinerator, all of which have environmental side effects.) Most food packaging will burn, but be sure to remove foil residue from the ashes. Eggshells burn in a hot fire and will eliminate a stinky mess in your trash bag. Any wrappings, plastic or not, that have contained meats should

Only two ways to dispose of trash

❏ Burn it

❏ Pack it out

be burned, or the rancid odor will draw bears and insects.

Should you have good luck fishing and keep a few for a meal, you'll be faced with the task of properly disposing of the offal and carcass. The very best way I know of accomplishing this is to clean the fish away from camp, place the remains in a visible place near the water's edge, and let the seagulls dispose of it. Chop any big carcass into sizes the birds can handle, or they'll drag it into the water, where it will sink. Seagulls won't dive for food. Should the gulls not appear, take the carcass into the woods and bury it in a shallow hole—but never near a campsite. Bears love ripe fish and you're just sending an invitation to them. Never throw fish carcasses in the shallow water near camp. Not only are they disgusting to look at but they'll foul the camp's drinking water.

Try not to disturb campsite vegetation, and confine your activities to the already impacted areas of the site. Campsites have a tendency toward "rural sprawl" when people continue to remove brush and trees and develop new tent sites.

Some folks go to great lengths to build elaborate camp furniture, which is a definite eyesore to the visitors who follow. If you need a table, just prop an overturned canoe on two logs, one front and back, and you'll have ample platform on which to prepare a meal.

Besides not doing obvious destruction to the camp, pay attention to the little things such as twist ties and cigarette butts. Pick them up. Don't leave trash in the fire grate. Leaving unburnt trash in the fire grate creates an unsightly, and perhaps unburnable, mess for the next campers if rain occurs in the interim. You hauled it in. You certainly can carry it out.

If you encounter someone else's trash, please pick it up and dispose of it properly. The rangers don't come along and perform maid service between campsite visitations. If you leave the trash, it will likely stay there for a very long time, probably gathering more garbage as lazy campers add to the pile. Many of the canoe country campsites are visited only once a year by U.S. or Canadian rangers, so it really is up to all of us to keep them clean.

Never cut live trees for wood. Don't break off boughs or strip birch bark, and don't trench around your tent. That shallow soil you see took ten thousand years to accumulate since the last glacier scoured the landscape clean. It is simply criminal to hasten erosion by such needless trenching. Buy yourself a good tent, seal the floor seams, and use a ground cloth, and you'll not need to trench. Place your ground cloth beneath the tent floor, making sure it is recessed at least six inches from the tent edge. If the ground cloth is exposed, water will collect between it and the tent floor, leading to possible leakage into the tent.

Watch your noise level. The best course is to leave radios at home; but if you insist on bringing one, turn down the volume. The greatest impact you will have on other visitors will be in the noise department. Sound carries inordinately far over water and on a quiet evening people as far as a half a mile away may be able to hear just about everything you say! Obviously, fireworks and firearms should also be left at home. You'll have no need for either.

The mark of a competent voyageur is a camp left cleaner than upon arrival and a small stack of ready firewood next to the fire grate for the next visitor. It is the way you would like to find a campsite, isn't it?

Once, midway through a month-long canoe trip, Mary Jo and I stumbled wearily into a campsite on an island on Quetico's Sturgeon Lake. We had fought big waves on this enormous lake all day and were nearly at the end of our strength when we arrived. Dragging the packs up to the fire ring took about as much energy as we had left. The little ring was clean, ashes shoveled out. Next to it was a neatly stacked pile of kindling. Though it had been a long time since this site had been used, some thoughtful camper had anticipated our arrival. Nothing, not even a twist tie, remained of the

A *good camper*

- ❏ Is careful about fire
- ❏ Keeps portages and campsites clean and neat
- ❏ Is quiet
- ❏ Leaves the campsite ready for next camper
- ❏ Disturbs the wilderness as little as possible

last occupants. After the tent was up and we had renewed our energy with dinner, I sat by the fire and silently thanked the last voyageurs who had passed this way. Their consideration had gone beyond cleanliness to the thoughtfulness of the pile of firewood. When we left the next morning, another pile of kindling lay neatly near the fire ring.

Are you looking for a very special campsite?

Once you leave the lakes nearest the entry points, where all campsites are likely to be frequently used, you have the opportunity to seek sites that can be quieter and cleaner than the norm. The technique is simple, the rewards are pleasant.

Take a look at a straightline path down the route you'll travel. Campsites within a short distance of that imaginary line are the ones more commonly used. Now look a bit to the left and right of that line. Even busy lakes often have winding bays that are a mile or more off this beaten path, many with BWCAW-designated campsites, or choice but seldom-used Quetico do-it-yourself locations. We've camped on busy lakes, a mile or two off the travel route, and seldom saw another person while enjoying a pristine campsite. The little extra work is worth the effort.

Likewise, taking one extra portage, especially on a dead-end route, off the travel circuit will frequently provide the serenity and cleanliness for which you came to this region. Putting a portage, or a long bay, between you and others helps to ensure privacy and a sense of solitude that will benefit you and other visitors. If possible, never camp within sight or hearing of others, for the benefit of both parties. And should a nearby group have a tape recorder and spend the evening playing "La Bamba" loudly (no kidding, this happened to us), you won't need to contemplate murder and mayhem as we did.

Bugs, Bears, and Other Travel Travails

The phone conversation wasn't going in the direction I had hoped. I had called a friend to hear about his recent bass fishing canoe trip, a trip he had taken to the same lake we were about to visit. What I heard instead was about the bugs—and it wasn't pretty.

"Had to leave a day early," he said. "Couldn't even eat outside. Never seen the bugs worse than that."

Great. What to do? We were all packed and ready to go. The fellow I talked to was experienced and not prone to complaining. If the insects had driven them home, were we wise to go? After all, if the trip wasn't to be enjoyable, why bother?

We went anyway. A shift in weather brought cool nights and breezy days. The campsite we chose took advantage of the wind to drive off the bugs, and the cool evenings reduced insect activity. We went prepared with proper clothing and ample bug dope. And the smallmouth bass fishing was superb, which for us goes a long way toward compensating for any adversity. All in all, the trip still ranks as one of our most pleasant.

When we conjure up visions of canoe trips, most of us picture the canoe country in only its best light: sunny days, blue skies, and crisp evenings around the fire. All of these things are true, sometimes. We often fail to acknowledge the

Be prepared for
- ❏ Wind
- ❏ Rain
- ❏ Pesky bears
- ❏ Mosquitoes
- ❏ Blackflies
- ❏ Ticks
- ❏ Unsafe water

very real other half of the picture: rain, wind, pesky bears, and evenings full of the whine of mosquitoes. If you go unprepared, such experiences can really dampen your canoe trip.

Preparing for the inevitable adversities is part experience and part common sense. I'll pass on our experience. You'll have to come up with your own common sense.

The challenges you'll most likely face are problem insects, poor weather, bad drinking water, and maybe camp-robbing black bears. Medical emergencies are less likely, but possible, especially if you haven't managed to exercise the common sense I referred to.

Biting insects are a pain

Let's be brutally honest here, folks. Bugs can be a major problem for some of us. Biting insects not only are a first-rate pain, they can affect your health. Mosquitoes, the most prevalent, are relatively harmless. But when present in large numbers, as they can be all summer during wet years, and certainly from late May into July every year, they can literally drive one insane. Blackflies, or gnats, follow roughly the same timetable as mosquitoes. They are just as annoying but come with the extra curse that some campers have mild allergic reactions to their bite. We're not talking life-threatening reactions, but some swelling near the bite and some aggravating itching. The big biters, horseflies and deerflies, pick up in midsummer, thriving during the hottest weather. Though not as great a problem as mosquitoes and blackflies, they are nonetheless something to wish only on your worst enemies.

Ticks and stinging insects (wasps, bees, hornets) are the only bugs that may lead to health problems. Anyone who has anaphylactic reactions to wasps, bees, or hornets must inform the entire party, at the beginning of the trip, what his or her reaction to such bites will be and where to find the allergic reaction medication. If you have someone who has suddenly passed out and is in shock, and no one knows where the medication is, well . . .

Both wood ticks and deer ticks are present in the canoe country. Wood ticks are generally nothing more than an itchy nuisance. Deer ticks can spread Lyme disease—which is serious business.

You can learn to handle insect problems routinely so that they need not adversely affect your adventure. Preparedness comes in three divisions: clothing, environmental factors, and chemicals. A combination of these three can be very effective.

No matter what the insect pest is, the best defense is sensible clothing. This includes long-sleeve shirts, trousers, and a hat. Although this seems almost too sensible to be even worth mentioning, we've seen countless canoeists red with welts and absolutely miserable, all because they wore little more than they would to the beach. Perhaps, like the monks who wore scratchy hair coats as a penance, these folks figure that misery is a necessary price for a canoe trip.

Light-colored garments, in a lightweight fabric with a tight weave, will thwart many insects. Light colors help you spot ticks crawling on you before they enter your clothing, and they reflect sunlight so the garments are bearable in weather that is at once both muggy and buggy. The tight weave will help put a bend in probing proboscises. Little things, like tight-fitting cuffs and a collar that is comfortable when buttoned shut, are important guards against blackflies, which like to crawl into your clothing before doing their dirty deed. When insects are at their peak, try tucking your pants legs into your boot tops or stockings. And since many insects, especially blackflies, like to bite your scalp, wear a hat. I'm not sure if any particular color repels insects, but I do know that light blue clothing seems to draw blackflies.

In the clothing category falls the head-net. If you are really bugged by insects (pun intended), you might want to consider purchasing one. In May and June we generally each

Wear protective clothing

- ❑ Long-sleeve shirts
- ❑ Long pants
- ❑ Hats
- ❑ Head-nets, if needed

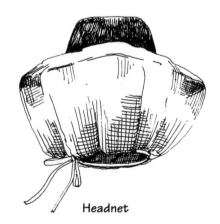

Headnet

Mosquitoes abound

❏ Near shallow water

❏ In still air

❏ In shade

❏ At dusk

❏ During early summer

Blackflies thrive

❏ Near moving water

❏ In full sun

❏ During early summer

carry one, though we seldom use it. When needed they are worth ten times their weight in gold. Ours are merely shapeless net bags. They fold up very small and weigh perhaps an ounce or two. When worn with a hat with an all-the-way-around brim, the netting will be kept away from your face and neck. If you let the net drape against you, the little vampires will simply stick their drilling rig right through to tap into you.

Environmental factors include three things: odors, location, and timing. Perfumed toiletries (deodorant, soap, shampoo, shaving cream, etc.) are extremely effective insect attractants, providing that's what you want to do. If not, I'd recommend leaving these things at home or purchasing unscented versions. These flowery products are particularly adept at attracting horseflies and deerflies. You could also try not bathing for the duration. It does help in driving off insects, honestly. But you might be pretty unpopular.

The second environmental factor is location. Obviously, if on the portage you must cross a swamp, one droning with mosquitoes, there just isn't much you can do about it. But you can choose where you camp. Mosquitoes lay their eggs in still, shallow water. If you have a choice, why camp near such conditions? Choose instead a spot near deep water, preferably where the breeze can get at you. Remember, only female mosquitoes bite, and they can't fly forward in a breeze stronger than eight miles per hour. A breeze-swept campsite can make conditions much more tolerable. Pay attention to wind direction when choosing a camp for an evening. Since this region has prevailing westerly winds, I often plan to camp accordingly.

Blackflies are worst near moving water. They like to lay their eggs in streams—ask any trout angler. In May and June, when blackflies are hatching, avoid camping near moving water, when possible. These little gnats also prefer full sun, whereas mosquitoes seem to prefer shade.

Finally, consider your timing. Mosquitoes and blackflies

are worst in the early summer. Maybe you want to avoid that period (though you'll miss out on the best fishing). Try to adjust your daily routine during the trip to avoid insect activity periods. Most people fish, paddle, swim, whatever, until evening and then settle down for dinner. That's exactly what the mosquitoes have in mind too. They are by far at their most active from an hour or so before sunset until full darkness arrives. We generally try to avoid any activity that requires standing around, such as cooking or eating, during this period. Instead, we eat early and then go fishing until after dark, or slide into the tent to read or nap. Once darkness falls, so does mosquito activity, and you can sit around the fire and enjoy the stars.

The big biting horseflies and deerflies can be a nuisance, but mostly when you are on the trail or sunbathing. Bug dope helps, but not much. Some flies seem impervious to these chemicals. Being on the water, in a breeze, is the best escape. Seldom are these flies a problem in cool weather or early and late in the day. Try to keep cool. Biting flies are attracted by body warmth and by the release of carbon dioxide—which is exactly what a hardworking portager emits. If these flies bother you, try traveling during the cooler periods of the day.

Ankle biters look much like an ash-gray, smaller version of the housefly. They drink bug dope for breakfast. Their bite feels like a red-hot poker. There is absolutely nothing you can do to escape them; they'll even follow you out onto the lake and dine on your ankles while hiding from the wind. A good defense is clothing. And patience. They present a problem for only about a week or ten days each summer. That period is usually in late June or early July. Fortunately, they are not found every year or in all locations. You pay your money and you take your chances . . .

Some campsites are more likely to have lots of flies than others, determined largely by the amount of use the site has seen. The more often the site has been used, the greater the

Horseflies and deerflies are annoying

- ❏ In warm weather
- ❏ At midday
- ❏ On the trail

odds of spilled Kool-Aid, improperly disposed-of food and fish entrails, and other slovenly behavior. Flies love that stuff. Just one more reason for looking for out-of-the-way campsites and for you to keep your own camp clean, clean, clean. Always wipe up food spills immediately. If you clean fish in or near camp, use your paddle to splash lots of water on the area to wash away any blood and slime.

Little details like this can make your stay (not to mention mine, should I happen to follow you) in this campsite much more pleasant.

Ticks can be a bother, but mostly in the itch department. Wood ticks, about an eighth of an inch in size, are large enough to spot and feel as they crawl on you. Although they can transmit illness, it is rare. Checking yourself over once a day is the only real means of catching them before they attach. When examining yourself for deer or wood ticks, pay close attention to the parts of your body covered with hair.

Deer ticks, however, are another matter entirely. They can be as tiny as the period at the end of this sentence. And they are the carriers of the serious, and occasionally fatal, Lyme disease. The good news is that both the deer tick and Lyme disease are still rare in the canoe country, although other parts of Minnesota (notably east central) are hotbeds of this tick and disease activity.

Because they are so small, deer ticks aren't often noticed until after they've attached themselves and become engorged. An engorged deer tick is still smaller than the average unengorged wood tick. Not every deer tick carries Lyme disease, nor is the disease transmitted instantly upon attachment. Removal of the tick up to twelve hours after attachment can still stop Lyme transmission, although the sooner you remove the tick, the better. A tick that is still moving about on you hasn't fed yet.

Remove attached ticks carefully. If you have a tweezers in your first aid kit (they're also found on many Swiss Army

Check carefully every day for ticks

knives), use it to grasp the tick as near as possible to its mouth (where it enters your skin). Pull gently but steadily outward. Whatever you do, don't squeeze the tick's abdomen. You can actually inject tick fluids, much as if it were a syringe, by squeezing the tick. Clean the bite area with soap and water or antibiotic solution.

Lyme disease symptoms appear three to thirty days after the bite and include a spreading rash, profound fatigue, flulike symptoms, and/or a stiff neck. More serious symptoms occur later on, often mimicking other diseases. Caught early, Lyme disease is easily treated with simple antibiotics.

Insect repellents can help

The final defense against biting insects are insect repellents. I choose these as a last resort because of the toxicity of these products. That said, I also wouldn't travel without them, especially because of deer ticks.

By far the most effective repellent ingredient is DEET (N,N-Diethyl-meta-Toluomide). Brand names are really irrelevant. DEET is DEET. It works on all ticks and biting insects, but is more effective against some than others. Blackflies seem the most immune to it. You'll find that varying brands, or formulas within same-brand products, contain different percentages of DEET. The major difference between a product that is thirty per cent DEET and one that is ninety per cent is not how well each repels insects, but how long it lasts. The lower the percentage, the more often you'll need to apply it.

Liquid repellents come in small two-ounce bottles and are generally over ninety per cent DEET. This formula is effective for applying to exposed skin, and the small size makes it easy for every party member to have a bottle in his or her pocket. Such formulas last up to ten hours per application. Lotions and creams contain less DEET, but some campers may find them more pleasant to apply. Sprays

Insect repellent with DEET

149

rarely contain over forty per cent DEET, but are very handy for applying to clothing, which is an effective way of "radiating" an aura of insect protection. Try to keep all repellents away from synthetic clothing, plastics, fishing line, and varnished items. Damage could occur.

For protection against deer ticks, apply liquid DEET to exposed skin and spray your clothing, especially your lower body, with a repellent that contains thirty to fifty-five per cent DEET. Less than thirty per cent DEET is not nearly as effective, and products containing more than fifty-five per cent DEET offer no additional protection while costing more. Another effective tick repellent is Permanone, a permethrin-based product. This can be applied only to clothing. The combination of DEET on your skin and Permanone on your clothing is perhaps the best protection. For what it is worth, government agencies consider DEET-based repellents safe for people of all ages when used according to instructions.

You should consider one other aspect when thinking about the battle of the bugs. What I have described here is a worst-case scenario. During the peak of insect activity, all is not miserable all day. You can have a wonderful canoe trip during the buggiest part of the season and avoid the crowds that traditionally visit the canoe country in August. Really, the most important factor in this battle is psychology. If you prepare yourself mentally for insects, decide that you aren't going to be annoyed by them, you'll have the situation well in hand before departure. A mental immunity is entirely possible to develop.

Wind, waves, and lightning

We addressed wind conditions a bit in a previous chapter; the cardinal rules are never to venture out into seas larger than you are capable of safely handling as well as always trying to quarter into, or run with, the waves. Traveling parallel to waves, by running in the troughs, can be done by the skilled, but is considerably more dangerous. Paddling near shore is always wise because waves diminish within yards of the shore as some of their energy is absorbed by the shallow lake bottom.

Traveling in thunderstorms is foolhardy. Lightning is attracted to the tallest object, which will be you, if you stay out on the lake under such conditions. If you must paddle when lightning is present, a margin of safety can be found by maintaining a distance from shore of forty yards. Further from shore than that, you become a target. Nearer to shore, lightning striking a nearby tree can easily jump to you. Forty yards out is far enough to avoid the lightning jump, and near enough so that the trees will be the tallest object and therefore the target. Don't sue me if you follow this advice and get fried. I still recommend getting off the water.

Since storms approach from the west, southwest, or northwest, any thunderheads you see that are directly north, south, or east of you will miss you. Should you see ominous thunderclouds west of you, be prepared to head for shore. Pay attention to rumbling and cloud speed so that you can allow for enough time to get to safety and perhaps string up a tarp to sit the storm out.

The most dangerous part of your canoe trip, other than the drive from home, comes during periods of lightning. More people have died of lightning strikes in the canoe country than from any other cause. Even if you have taken the precaution of getting off the water, you are not completely safe. Never sit, or camp beneath, tall trees. Those ancient monarch pines of the forest may be impressive to look at, but they are also effective lightning rods. Keep in mind that the root system can extend for long distances from the trunk and they can easily transmit fatal amounts of electricity to campers sleeping or sitting on those roots. Of course the odds are very much in your favor that lightning will not strike you, or even strke near you, but minimize your chances by choosing tent sites carefully.

Your water supply is important

Another hazard you may have heard of is the intestinal illness giardiasis, commonly known as giardia. Giardia is passed on through drinking contaminated water. The actual "bug" is spread by beavers, as well as by the contamination of water by human or pet excrement. This disease is manifested by severe stomach cramps and a world-class case of diarrhea. Giardia doesn't happen overnight. If you have cramps your first day out, it is much more likely you that didn't drink enough water and are dehydrated, or that you ate too much greasy food at that last hamburger place on your way up. Symptoms show up no earlier than four or five days after ingestion and may take a week or two to develop.

The incidence of giardia is fairly low, and the disease is nothing new. It has been present in the canoe country for a very long time, but there has been much more awareness about it in recent years.

You can eliminate the chances of contracting giardia by filtering all your water, or by boiling it for three to five minutes. By being careful where you take your water, you can possibly get by without treatment. First, never take water from near beaver lodges or dams. Also, avoid water in streams or along windblown shorelines. In both cases, if giardia is present, the stirring action of moving water will suspend it, making picking it up much more likely. Most experienced voyageurs routinely drink water without any treatment and have gone years without contracting giardia. Some doctors feel that an immunity can be built up by a succession of minor bouts with this bug.

I consider it far more important to avoid getting dehydrated when canoeing and portaging, and dehydration is much more likely if you must stop to boil or filter water each time you get thirsty—human nature being what it is, you'll probably not stop to treat and drink water often enough.

Actually, proper hydration requires drinking water BEFORE you become too thirsty.

When cooking, we'll be boiling the water anyway, so we aren't overly cautious with the water source. For drinking water to keep in camp, we paddle a fair distance out into the lake and fill a water bag to hang in the shade of a tree back in camp. This becomes our water source for drinking, brushing our teeth, and the like. While traveling, we exercise the same caution by waiting until we are in the middle of the lake to fill our water bottles. To eliminate surface water, plunge your water bottle upside down to arm's length below the surface, then tip it upright. Most creepy-crawly things are in the surface film.

To be fair, the Forest Service recommends treating all water. If they didn't, and someone got sick, they'd probably end up being sued. So I'll recommend the same thing. We don't treat our own water. You can do as you wish, but to be as safe as possible, boil or filter it. Of course, better not go swimming then either, since you might get some water on your lips and accidentally swallow it. My feeling is that you have to accept some risks while in the wilderness.

A good first aid kit is a must

You may not need it often, but to travel without one is simply asking for trouble. Stuff some extra aspirin and Band-Aids into the kit. These will be the items most often needed. Sinus or cold pills are also a good addition, since many folks develop sinus problems from sleeping on the ground in the cool night air. Solutions for treating sunburn and insects bites can also save a lot of discomfort. At least one person in your party should be familiar with first aid practices. First aid is too important a subject to treat briefly here. Attend an accredited first aid course, buy a good book on the subject, or talk a medic or doctor friend into going along on the trip. Should there be a really serious emergency on your trip, you must handle the

First aid essentials

❏ Carry a well-stocked first aid kit

❏ Take an accredited first aid course

❏ Study and take along a good first aid book

situation wisely and calmly. The odds of a ranger with a radio being anywhere near you at such a time are extremely low. If the situation is not life threatening, the best bet is to administer first aid and begin to transport the injured person out. If you encounter other parties who can travel faster and are also heading toward help, WRITE all pertinent information down (names, home addresses, type of injury or illness, where you are located, which route you'll be traveling, where you plan on exiting) and ask them to deliver it to the Forest Service or local sheriff's office. Never assume, having done this, that the message has reached help. Repeat it with other parties, but act as if you are the sole source of aid until, and maybe unless, qualified authorities arrive.

Even then, evacuation will likely be via motorless ground transport, just as you are already traveling, unless the problem is truly life threatening. Only in such cases do the authorities authorize motor use or air traffic into the wilderness. And don't be surprised if you get a bill for the search and rescue services.

It is always smart to leave a travel itinerary with the nearest ranger's office, or someone at home, before embarking. It is also wise to advise those waiting for you at home that sometimes wind and weather mean you may be late in getting out. Remind them that this possibility exists, that being late doesn't always mean something bad has happened, and that they should wait a reasonable period before calling authorities. It might also be wise to leave at home the telephone number of the Forest Service or Quetico Park office.

Most accidents in the canoe country are the direct result of foolish risks. Common hazards are paddling without wearing a PFD, diving off high cliffs while swimming, running whitewater, and climbing trees. It is so simple to avoid these risks that one wonders why people continue to take chances. Remember, you are a long way from help, and behavior that you might not have considered risky elsewhere

Always, always, always wear a life jacket

should be reevaluated here. Keep an eye on other members of your party. If they hurt themselves, YOU will be the one to carry them out.

Beware the pesky bear

Perhaps the most realistic "problem" you will encounter is raids by black bears. On popular lakes within the BWCAW and Quetico it is almost a given that bears will visit, especially if the berry crop has been bad and the bruins are getting hungry. Your first defense is to ask the local rangers which areas have been experiencing problems and then try to avoid those spots.

Your second defense is to keep your camp clean and odor-free, and combine that with storing your food out of the reach of bears. This should extend to nonfood items that may smell good to bears, such as toothpaste, breath mints, and such. Leaving those in your tent is extending an invitation to bears to come on in.

You should know that black bears aren't dangerous. I didn't say they aren't potentially dangerous—for they are large, strong animals equipped with all kinds of havoc-raising tools such as teeth and claws. But being vicious just isn't in their nature. When confronted, even in your campsite as it stands over your food pack, a black bear will almost always back down. When bears exhibit aggressive behavior it is because careless campers have allowed them to obtain food—and black bears aren't stupid. They'll continue to bluff frightened campers because they know the technique works. They even pass it on to their offspring. Never, never, never, let a bear leave camp with your chow. You'll only be adding to the problem.

It is important that you not let bears have your food because ultimately it may lead to the bear's being destroyed. You can stop this chain of tragedy by practicing good bear-aversion techniques. This is the bear's home. Bad behavior

Noisemakers

on its part, like that of humans, is the result of repeated conditioning that has allowed the bear to get away with its pilfering. Problem bears are human-created, not born.

Bears can be driven off through a combination of yelling, stone-tossing, pot-banging, and other eccentric behavior designed to let the big panhandler know that you want the food more than he does. Bears would make good gamblers. They take a look at the odds and then go for it. If they figure they'll get brained with a rock, they'll leave. If they bet they can scare you, they'll try it. Always give the animal an escape route so it doesn't feel inordinately threatened. If you are in a camp that is being repeatedly harassed by bears, grab your food pack during a lull and move on.

Most of the time you can avoid problems by hanging your food out of harm's way. Since a bear standing on its hind legs can reach up to eight feet off the ground, that is the very minimum distance you should suspend your pack. Ten feet is even better. It must also be a safe distance from the trunk of the tree. Bears can hug the tree and still reach out at least four feet. Allow at least six feet. They also can lie on a branch and reach down quite far (even on a branch of surprisingly small diameter). Four feet here wouldn't be any too great a gap, and I'd allow for more, when possible.

Many campsites offer suitable branches from which to suspend packs. Use a stout nylon rope of at least three-eights of an inch diameter. Tie a rock to one end (or put a rock in a nylon sack and tie that to the rope) and toss it over the branch. You really can't hang a pack too high. Sometimes finding a good branch, especially one that allows the pack to be a sufficient distance from the tree trunk is difficult. In that case, attach a second rope to the pack, and after hoisting the food well off the ground with the first rope, use the second rope to pull the pack away from the tree. (The second rope can be a parachute cord since its primary duty is only to swing the pack out.) It often helps to throw this second rope over a branch of another nearby tree so that when you tighten it the pack will be swung not only away from the first tree but upward as well. You may need to toss the first rope over a branch farther up in the tree than you normally might choose, because in order to swing the pack out, you need some slack in the first rope between the branch and the pack to make it possible to pull the pack out with the second rope. With two ropes, using this technique, you can hang a food pack anywhere in the canoe country.

Always find a good spot to hang your pack when you first make camp. Doing it right takes time, and if you wait until bedtime you'll find the job frustrating, if not impossible, in the growing darkness. Test the branch for strength by gingerly pulling straight down on the rope. Be prepared to run if you hear the branch cracking. You want to find out if the system will work while you have time to move it, not in the dark.

If you have a hard time getting the pack high enough, due to its weight, have another person help push it up with a pole or canoe paddle. Some folks carry pulleys. These work well and avoid rope scars on trees, but are extra weight to carry. One reason I recommend nylon rope versus cotton, hemp, or polypropylene is that nylon's surface is much slicker and it slides more easily over the branch as you pull. If your food packs are kept to a reasonable weight, two people should have no problem when working together hanging the packs.

Some folks don't believe in hanging food packs. They put them in their canoe and float it out into the lake, store the packs under an overturned canoe, or take the packs well away from camp and put them on the water's edge. These techniques may work well for a while but eventually they will fail. If a bear doesn't swim out, flip over, or stumble across packs stored in this manner, some other critter will. Food packs on the ground are particularly susceptible to damage from mice and chipmunks—and you'd be amazed at just how much damage can occur.

Hang food packs
ten feet above ground

Some campsites have poles lashed between two trees for hanging food packs. I've never seen one yet that got the packs far enough off the ground, nor put enough space between the packs and the tree trunks. Imagine yourself as a bear and, while on the ground, hook one leg and arm around the tree and reach out as far as you can with the other arm. If you can stretch to the middle of the pole, so can a bear. Find a suitable tree instead.

Two fellows who flagged us down when we were rangers on Crooked Lake told us a particularly sad story. Seems they hung their packs none too well and about sunrise B'rer Bruin came along and made off with one of them. As they lay in their tent at first light, they heard a loud thunk. Peering out the tent door, they saw a large black bear dragging off one of their two packs. They raced outside, hollered at the bear, and when it made a bluffing grunt and lunge, retreated in terror.

"The really sad thing," one of them said as they told the story, "is that the bear took the wrong pack. He left our food pack and made off with all of our fishing equipment, about fifteen hundred bucks worth of camera gear, and our stove and cook kit. We have plenty of food, just nothing to cook it in. And our car keys and wallets were also in that pack."

They went on to ask us if they thought there was anything we could do to get their pack back. Problem was, they left that site, some four or five portages away, without really searching for that pack. I urged them to return the next morning to search for their equipment, and in the meantime we'd loan them some cooking gear. I figured that the bear had little use for the camera gear and car keys, though it might be interested in their fishing tackle, seeing as how bears love to eat fish.

"I wonder why the bear took that pack?" I asked rather rhetorically.

"Um, well, we left some gorp in it. Forgot about it from our lunch break. Guess we'll never do that again."

Amen. Bears can be a nuisance, but as this story relates, most successful raids are the result of poor hanging techniques or silly mistakes. Fortunately, both of these causes can be eliminated.

Though this whole chapter has been about some of the woes and dangers you might encounter in the canoe country, don't let the tone worry you. "Adventure" happens only to the unprepared or careless. Most of your trip will be filled with the glories you sought, and your memories will reflect those wonderful moments. The stars will shine brightly, the wind will be calm, and the lonely yodel of the loon will sing you to sleep.

Had we worried overly about the insect report in that phone conversation at the beginning of this chapter, we might not have gone. What a mistake that would have been. Though the canoe country can indeed force you to endure some hardship, though the bosom of nature can sometimes be stony, these things are but a test. For when you combine good sense and careful preparation with practiced skill, the canoe country will show to you the loveliest it has to offer.

And that is well worth the price.

Don't worry about the wilderness

I wasn't kidding when I said the drive to your entry point was the most dangerous part of your trip. The canoe country isn't full of malevolent spirits (though some mischievous ones exist, as the Ojibwa knew). Nor are the animals dangerous.

As I was writing this chapter I coincidentally received a call from an old high school friend of Mary Jo. This woman, who is a fairly typical urbanite, was planning her family's first camping trip to northern Minnesota and very seriously asked me if I thought the bears would attack and eat her or her children. She was equally concerned about wolves.

Put such thoughts to rest. These animals could be dangerous if they wanted to be. They just don't want to be.

Bears are likely to bluff you, but will back down. And wolves will avoid you like the plague—which the human race has been to them all through history. Old woodsmen consider the moose the most dangerous animal in the north woods, but only during the rut (autumn) when bulls will challenge just about anything that moves. You'd have to be looking for trouble, though, to find it, or spend a lifetime in the woods to have it happen by chance.

My wife's friend was skeptical but relieved at my answer. She said she hoped her young children would adapt to sleeping in a tent and related that her son, on his first night in a tent the previous summer, had struggled and finally bit his mom. When I told her that her children sounded more dangerous to me than the forest animals, she quickly ended our conversation. The truth hurts.

Wind and weather are your biggest risks in the wilderness. Pay attention, wear a PFD, and use common sense. Then be careful on the drive back to your home.

Wilderness Wildlife

Basswood River churned noisily over the lower falls as we paddled upstream toward Wheelbarrow Portage. A calm, warm day lay heavy on the canoe country, blue skies punctuated with white comma clouds.

We stroked along just outside the emerald horsetail reeds a few yards from shore, the only sound our slightly swishing paddles. Rounding a point, both Mary Jo and I suddenly back-paddled, halting the canoe in a quiet hurry. Ahead, on the water's edge and ankle deep, stood two whitetail fawns, each still speckled with infant camouflage, tawny miniature deer against a dark forest background.

We sat silently, smiling, watching the deer watch us. When it became apparent to them that we posed no threat, they ambled comfortably along the shore, feeding, drinking, and twitching their ears. Slowly I eased my camera from a pack and took some photos. After five minutes we backed away as noiselessly as we had appeared and left them to do whatever fawn deer do on such a lovely summer day.

Spotting wildlife ranks high on the list of hoped-for experiences for visitors to the canoe country. To those who come from distant parts of the country, or are urbanites, the wildlife of the canoe country is even more special. No one will ever forget a first encounter with a moose, nor the sight of a bald eagle wheeling overhead.

An encounter with wildlife will be a highlight of your camping trip

Most wildlife observations are merely happenstance. But you can do things to increase your odds of close encounters of the furry or feathery kind.

Increase your odds of seeing wildlife

The single most important thing one can do to view more wildlife is to travel quietly. Those who haven't spent much time in the woods greatly underestimate the sense of hearing with which our fellow creatures are endowed. Add the fact that the canoe country is a watery-wilderness, where sound travels far and quickly. Banging canoes on portage landings and talking loudly rapidly alerts animals to your presence, causing them to fade quietly into the protection of heavy cover. And because noise generally is inherent in larger groups, small parties are much more likely to see the canoe country's residents.

Beyond being quiet, it is extremely helpful to paddle near shore. Edge habitats are especially attractive to wildlife for many reasons, depending upon species. But the most well-defined "edge" in the canoe country is the one where water meets the forest, and along that edge is the best place to travel. Here you may see moose or deer feeding or escaping insects, and mink and otter travel the shorelines of lakes and streams to feed. Birds of prey, such as bald eagles and osprey, perch in water's edge trees to watch for feeding opportunities. It is a sure bet as well that shallow, fertile lakes and creeks will provide many more opportunities to watch wildlife than can be found on some of the wilderness's big, sterile bodies of open water.

Third, you must be observant, must develop what has been called the "hunter's eye." The hunter's eye is simply the art of seeing something that is different than the surroundings, noticing movement or an unusual shape. Though wildlife is often very well camouflaged, it still is but a disguise. They are not invisible. A small flicker in the brush

To see more wildlife

❏ Travel quietly

❏ Paddle near shore

❏ Be observant

❏ Listen carefully

❏ Watch for signs

❏ Look at dawn and dusk

along a stream may be a gray jay, but it could also be the twitching of a deer tail or a moose ear. Once you observe an abnormality, pause and study it. If you are patient, the creature will inevitably move. And when it does, it is amazing how quickly you pick out the full body shape: the legs and head of the moose miraculously sprout before your very eyes where only moments ago you saw just a flicker and what appeared to be a tangle of trees.

Shape can be a giveaway. I recall spotting a dark hump in a back bay of Quetico's Anubis Lake, perhaps a half mile away from us as we paddled north. It could have been a glacial erratic, and no doubt the party paddling down the lake in front of us thought it was just such a boulder. But as I studied it, it seemed inordinately dark, somehow different that the other rocks in the area. Judging the breeze carefully so that we could approach the hump from downwind, Mary Jo and I paddled quietly up the bay. As we neared, we noticed that occasionally the hump moved or changed shape. Finally, we knew that what we were watching was an almost completely submerged bull moose, contentedly feeding on water lilies and cooling off on a hot, buggy day. Each time its head went underwater, we paddled quickly forward, pausing when it came up. We sneaked to within twenty yards this way and then paused to admire this great beast.

I'm sure the party that had preceded us would have relished this sight as much as we did, and yet they paddled right by without so much as a glance. Being observant is critical, and so is developing the hunter's eye. For instance, I always pause for a double take whenever I spot a horizontal line along and above the shoreline or in the forest. While such a line could be a fallen tree or a rock, the majority of lines in the forest are vertical. The odds are then that in an area without human contrivances, the horizontal lines are the backs of large animals such as deer, moose, or bear.

It pays to note whether movement is in unison with that of wind in tree branches or on water. Often the only way to

Moose

Otter

distinguish between the chop on the lake of a breezy day and a playful otter swimming amidst that chop is to pay attention to the movement of the water and its direction. Anything unusual could very well be the wildlife you are hoping to see.

Don't forget that we need not see wildlife to know they are around. Bashful, to say the least, particular species may not come into view but many will leave signs of their passing for us to read. Piles of crayfish shells probably mean an otter dined at that spot. Sand beaches are great places to watch for the tracks of shorebirds and mammals, big and small. Moose tracks on portages are very visible, but many people miss the smaller tracks of the white-tailed deer. If you are going to be in the area awhile, and really want to see wildlife, returning to those spots where you've seen droppings or tracks and waiting patiently may pay dividends.

Serious students of wildlife may want to bring their full-size binoculars on their trip, such as an 8x40 power model. Most of us can probably make do with the smaller pocket-size binoculars of a similar power. They aren't as easy to hold, nor are they as efficient in low light, but they can really help in identifying species.

Finally, be out and about when the birds and animals are. Generally, the odds are greatest for wildlife watching in the morning or at dusk.

Mammals of the canoe country

Wolves are the glamour mammal of the canoe country, but unfortunately about the only visible signs you're likely to see of the reclusive timber wolf are their tracks and droppings.

Wolf scat is not often seen fresh, but dried scat, usually left behind from the previous winter, can be seen fairly frequently once you know what you are looking for. When wolves consume a moose or deer during the winter, they devour nearly the entire animal. That means the hide too is digested, but the hair of their dinner is passed through; when seen dried on a summer day, it looks like a loosely twisted chunk of rope about five inches long and an inch or so thick. The studious may even be able to tell whether the wolf had eaten moose or deer by an examination of the hair. Portages, on early season canoe trips before they have been heavily trodden, or the tops of high ridges (where you've climbed for the view and the blueberries!) are the best places to watch for wolf droppings.

The odds are much greater that you'll hear a wolf than see one, and the odds of hearing one aren't all that great. Perhaps because hearing wolves is rare, the experience is so exciting. I've heard wolves howl an hour or so after complete darkness, and again just at sunrise, particularly on rainy days. I guess they howled near me during the middle of the night as well, but little can be heard over my snoring.

Wolf

Moose and deer are the most commonly spotted large mammals, and the chances for seeing either are best near water. Most folks know that moose love to feed on aquatic plants during the summer, but I have seen many white-tailed deer doing the same over the years. As the forest matures in the canoe country, the whitetail population continues to drop because they favor young forests. In those areas of the Boundary Waters that were logged relatively near to their inclusion to the wilderness in 1978, fair white-tail populations still exist. Some white-tailed deer roam the hills of the Man Chain lakes in the Quetico and in the far northeast and northwest parts of the park, where logging has occurred within or near its borders. Moose are scattered throughout the region and concentrate wherever good habitat exists. For instance, the large burned-over area near Camel and Metacryst lakes in the Quetico has an abundance of moose because they enjoy the young, succulent browse that sprouts after a fire.

Slow waterways are always good places to watch for these monster deer, but you need to travel quietly. Busy routes

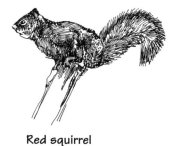

Red squirrel

usually result in fewer moose sightings because of heavy traffic. Watch for moose at dawn and dusk and, on very hot midsummer days, all day long in shallow back bays, where they can submerge themselves to stay cool and feed at the same time.

There are plenty of mice and voles, as well as red squirrels and chipmunks (both eastern and least) to keep you company in camp. Don't feed these little scamps, because they can quickly become campsite pests and can do nearly as much damage to your food pack as can a bear. Even hanging your pack doesn't help, because they'll just scoot right down the rope, crawl into the pack, and eat their way back out.

Speaking of bears, it is a fair bet that most campers would rather not see a black bear on their canoe trip for the simple reason that most sightings involve the bear trying to swipe food. Still, bears are magnificent animals and a lot of fun to watch. We've seen them far out in the middle of large lakes on two different occasions, swimming their way to, you guessed it, island campsites to check out whether or not the campers there figured a little water surrounding them meant they didn't have to hang their food packs. In a few places in the canoe country, black bears gather to harvest suckers as they spawn in the spring, grabbing fish from the shallow creeks in much the same way as their bigger cousins, the brown bears, catch salmon. It is quite a sight to see.

Black bear

I wish I could tell you where to see otters, but I have a feeling that when you encounter otters it is really more their decision than yours. They can appear anywhere, are very curious, and will approach you if you are quiet and remain still; and they're enormously playful and fun to watch. We've seen them surface like periscopes, dive from cliffs, and even come up and inspect our tent in the middle of the night. You'll be most likely to see otters, as well as mink and weasels, if you paddle near the shore of quiet lakes and streams.

Boreal birds

Avid birders are in for a treat when visiting the canoe country. The Boundary Waters and Quetico are very special for those interested in viewing boreal birds, such as the twenty-seven species of wood warblers and a host of boreal specialists like the flycatchers and the black-backed woodpecker that call the area home. Bring your bird book and binoculars and be out in the early morning hours.

Many campers have encountered the precocious gray jay, also known as the Canada jay. Because of their daring propensity to glide noiselessly into campsites and make off with bits of flapjacks or other morsels, this friendly jay is also known as the "camp robber." Its other common name, whiskey jack, is derived from the Ojibwa *wis-ka-tjon*. If you sit still, these bold birds will often hop to within inches of you, and it is not unheard of to have one sit atop your hat.

Two types of grouse are in the canoe country, the common ruffed grouse and the rarer spruce grouse. Odds are a quiet walker will see these birds on portages. Because most portage trails wind their way along the upland deciduous forests, ruffed grouse are more commonly spotted in this, their preferred habitat; the spruce grouse prefers dense stands of conifers. Spruce grouse are always darker and usually smaller than their close relative and do not have the black-banded tail for which the ruffed grouse is known. Since they are remarkably tame in the canoe country, you might be able to get near enough to see the red band over the spruce grouse's eye that definitely sets it apart from the ruffed grouse.

Ruffed grouse

While I've only spotted a few black-backed woodpeckers over the years, the larger pileated woodpecker is fairly common and easily seen if you follow the reverberating sound this crow-size bird makes as it raps on trees. Hairy and downy woodpeckers can be found in much the same way.

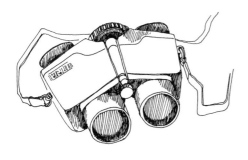

Binoculars

Often difficult to approach, the great blue heron is a common bird to this wilderness. If one spots you before you see it, which is almost always, it'll stretch out its neck and go absolutely rigid. The gray coloration and lack of motion makes it very hard to spot. Watch for them in shallow waters and marshy areas where they wade along on their spindly legs, looking for frogs and minnows. While you're there, keep your eyes open for a rich brown bird about two feet long with its pointy bill and head angled straight to the sky. That'll be the American bittern, which, like its cousin the great blue heron, freezes when it is suddenly surprised. They often make a booming sound, sort of a "boom ba-doom," back in the marshes.

Numerous hawks as well as bald eagles and osprey find the living good in the quiet canoe country. While you may spot these birds perched along shore, more commonly you'll see them soaring. Another large soaring bird in this country is the turkey vulture; when you see it from a distance, it is possible to confuse it with an immature eagle, which lacks the distinctive white head and rump of its parents.

The surest way to identify these three large soaring birds when their coloration isn't visible is to watch the position of the outstretched wings. Eagles soar with wings in nearly a flat plane, although very strong winds will force even their powerful wings slightly upwards. The turkey vulture soars with its wings in a shallow V shape, and it usually has the primaries at the tips of its wings separated so that these feathers look like fingers. Vultures also have a very short neck compared to eagles.

The osprey isn't as large as either of these birds, but if size isn't enough to distinguish them, watch their wings. When they soar, their wing tips are arched downward in a shallow upside down W shape. Watch for the nests of eagles and ospreys in large pines on, or within sight of, the shore. Eagle nests are usually part way down the tree from the top, but many ospreys nest almost at the very tip of the tree.

You'll likely hear owls in the dark forest, but because of their nocturnal habits, you probably won't see any. The only time I clearly saw an owl in the summer was while sitting on the latrine after dark. It swooped down and very nearly took my hat off. I suppose it saw my head moving and mistook it for a grouse or hare. That'll give you something to think about next time you visit the latrine after dark.

Of course you'll likely see loons, as well as mergansers. A fair number of waterfowl also breed in the canoe country, the most common being mallards and black ducks, as well as a few diving duck species such as the ringneck.

Along with the thrill of watching the canoe country natives, for this is truly their home, not ours, comes the responsibility to minimize your impact upon them. The cumulative effects of repeated encounters with humans can cause some less-tolerant species to actually move out of an area that is prime habitat for them, and even those who will tolerate our visits can be stressed by those encounters. Most creatures' lives revolve around two activities: feeding and reproducing. Each time we disrupt their feeding, or interfere with their ability to care for young ones, we cause stress. And stressed animals and birds have lower survival rates.

So don't push that moose by approaching so near it bolts for cover. If the eagles you are watching are forced to fly from their nest, or disrupt their fishing, they will be less capable of caring for their young. Stop approaching an animal that displays signs of fright or agitation, such as nervous movement, tenseness in the muscles, stamping of feet, or repeated head movement with quick, furtive glances toward you. If they continue to behave in a relatively normal manner, enjoy the view and then leave quietly.

Merganser family

Professional wildlife photographers follow a simple rule that could apply to wildlife watchers as well: the welfare of the subject is more important than the photograph.

Keep quiet, travel near shore, be observant, and respect wildlife's space and needs. These guidelines, and a fair amount of luck, will provide you with pleasant memories of the magnificent canoe country's bountiful wildlife.

Wildlife photography

Photographing wildlife and scenery is a wonderful pastime on your canoe trip. You won't have the luxury, however, of carrying all the camera gear you own, since weight and space quickly becomes a factor.

One SLR camera body and two zoom lenses will fit the bill for just about all your needs. My first choice in lenses is a 35-105 zoom, which gives you a moderate wide-angle at the short end for scenic shots and a short telephoto for cropping scenes or for portraits. An 80-210 zoom, or some similar configuration, gives you enough length to reach out and capture wildlife. If I were to bring one more lens, it would be a 24 or 28mm wide-angle model.

The best of all films for reproduction are tight-grained, slow speed slide films, such as Kodachrome 64—long the choice of professional photographers. Fujichrome 100 is an excellent choice too. If you need a faster film, try Kodachrome 200. If you have no intention of selling photos to publishers, you can shoot print film, which is available in very fast speeds—up to 1000 ISO. Still, the slower the film (smaller the number), the less grain (more sharpness) you'll notice in the finished photographs. A 200 ISO print film would be a good all-around choice.

Camera gear needs protection from bumps and water, but it should't be so elaborate that you'll not hassle with freeing it for those quick shots. See "Good Gear = Good Trip" for more information about packing cameras.

Compact point-and-shoot cameras, especially those with a built-in short zoom lens, take wonderful photos and may be the best choice for many canoeists.

Additional
Resources

On Wilderness

Less than a half a century ago, the banner of developers plying their trade on the edge of the Quetico-Superior Wilderness was "A Road to Every Lake." A frightening thought.

Look at a map of the canoe country. No other place on the planet offers such a canoeists' mecca. Thousands of lakes, hundreds of miles of rivers, all linked by connecting portage trails through almost two and a half million acres of boreal forest. This resource is an international treasure, as unique as the Everglades, as spectacular as the Rockies.

The American half, the Boundary Waters Canoe Area Wilderness (BWCAW), is the most visited segment of the national wilderness system. It is one of the last substantial unbroken portions of the once vast eastern forest, and is the largest wilderness east of the Rockies. Sitting atop the oldest exposed rock in the world, this magnificent region is the southern edge of the vast Canadian Shield, that dome of Precambrian earth crust that sweeps from here north and east across Canada. Scoured clean by glaciers ten thousand years ago, the region evolved from a wet and rocky tundra to the boreal woodland dominated by a climax forest of towering white and Norway pines.

The early human history of this lakeland wilderness is that of hunter-gatherers. Traveling by canoe, mostly in family groups, they hunted the region's large game, primarily moose and woodland caribou, and gathered the bountiful wild rice and a variety of berries. They also left behind the haunting rock paintings, known as pictographs, that dot the canoe country rocks with their red ochre mystery.

When the voyageurs traveled the same portages as the Indians, the same portages as you will travel, they came to extract this area's wealth of furs, particularly the luxurious pelt of the beaver, as well as to use it as a route to even greater fur wealth to the northwest. Though less damaging to the culture of the native peoples than later visitors, they did alter the Indian lifestyle by encouraging a switch from seasonal resource use to full-time trapping. The voyageur era continued until the mid-1800s, when fashion changes and a financial depression made furs less valuable. By then the fur resource was largely depleted. Perhaps the last voyageur tromped up the Horse Portage around the roaring Basswood River as recently as in the 1850s, on his way to the last Hudson Bay Company's fur-trading post to operate on Lake Superior, the Michipicoten House, which closed its doors for good in 1904.

More changes have occurred in the canoe country in the last one hundred years than in thousands of years' previous history. Loggers came to extract the wealth of pine, removing the majority of it on the American side before 1920. Parts of the Quetico were also logged, some into very recent times, but the interior of that park still contains significant stands of pines, some over three hundred years old.

In 1909 Quetico was declared a provincial forest reserve; and the Superior National Forest, which is the largest in the contiguous forty-eight states and which contains the present BWCAW, was created on the American side. Since that time both halves of this wilderness have enjoyed various sorts of legal protection.

The history of official wilderness has been convoluted and contentious. In 1922 Arthur Carhart, then a United States Forest Service landscape architect, recommended that the northern half of the Superior National Forest be forever roadless. Unfortunately, the Forest Service didn't listen to Carhart. It bowed, instead, to the wishes of developers, and drew up an expansive road-building plan. Political pressure from the Izaak Walton League of America, a pioneer conservation group, helped to make the Forest Service abandon its aggressive road-building plans. After much struggle, the Thye-Blatnick Act of 1948 was passed, allowing the Forest Service to acquire many of the resorts and inholdings (privately owned lands) within the wilderness to preserve its character. In 1949, in response to increasingly disruptive floatplane flights, and despite stiff opposition from local concerns, an executive order from the president of the United States, the first of its type in the world, prohibited airplanes from flying below four thousand feet over the wilderness or landing within it. Ontario authorities adopted a landing ban shortly thereafter, although no airspace ban has been enacted.

The battle between developers and wilderness aficionados heated up even more with the signing of the 1964

Wilderness Act, which pitted neighbor against neighbor, northern Minnesota against the south, customer against outfitter. The battle raged over outboard motor use and snowmobiles, until President Carter signed Public Law 95-495 on October 21, 1978. Since enactment of this legislation, the BWCAW has existed in its present form: roadless, largely motorless, wilderness. Quetico's status was changed shortly thereafter to a wilderness designation.

Wilderness today exists only where protected by law. But wilderness designation is a mixed blessing, for while it safeguards a region from development, it also acts as a magnet to lure many visitors. In each of the two wilderness areas, the American side managed by the Forest Service and Quetico managed by the Ontario Ministry of Natural Resources, visitor levels are controlled through an elaborate system of entry permits and restrictions on the type of use and equipment allowed within. But some 180,000 people visit the BWCAW each year on overnight trips. And many others make day visits. Quetico Provincial Park allows fewer visitors, and use levels are less than one-fifth that of the BWCAW for overnight stays. Lack of easy access makes day use there more difficult.

Most efforts in wilderness management center on these visitors with minimal management of the natural resources. Wildfire, for instance, has returned to its significant natural role in forest evolution, at least on the United States side, where naturally occurring fires are allowed to burn within specific guidelines. By and large, the wildlife and forest maintain themselves as they always have, although acid rain and toxic mercury deposited from airborne sources loom as an imposing threat, and the woodland caribou is extinct here thanks to the loggers and the human-caused fires that consumed caribou food as they ripped through the logging slash. Logging also made the habitat more favorable for white-tailed deer, which carried into the region a parasite fatal to caribou.

Wilderness is not solely for human use. Wilderness must exist as a place where ecosystems can continue to function largely unchanged, where evolution can continue to work. To imagine that such a place exists only for human pleasure, or that human recreation is its highest value, only perpetuates the egocentric philosophy that has led to so much of this world's destruction. Wilderness serves to teach our race humility, and gives us a place to practice it.

Today, the canoe country is a jewel, some of it never sullied, some of it reclaimed from the logging, mining, and resorting claims that had sprung up within the interior. Timber wolves stalk through the forest. Bald eagles and osprey swoop on unsuspecting fish. Moose and white-tailed deer, beavers and bears, otters and owls call this place home. Through it all human visitors come to answer the beckoning call of another age, to walk the portages of the Ojibwa and voyageurs, hoping to find within themselves a tangible link to our primordial past.

Listen for the pulse of the canoe country in the slow heaving of a quiet lake, and in the adrenaline rush of whitewater. Pause to hear its breathing in the branches of a pine. And listen to your own heart and mind, uncluttered for awhile, away from the din of our modern world. Wilderness travel means physical exertion and challenge, it means meeting wilderness on its own terms, not in an effort to conquer nature, but to exist at its level. When the wilderness challenges you, dig deeply for the inner reserve that is within us all. Meet the terms of nature, which, though sometimes harsh, are never malevolent.

Spare a moment's thought for those far-sighted people whose diligent work through much of this century stopped the "Road to Every Lake" dream of those whose hearts beat only to the sound of jingling coins. Remember, however, that the battle is never over; new pressures on the wilderness arise every year, and nothing, not even federal legislation, is sacrosanct.

Fishing the Canoe Country

To many folks, a trip to the canoe country also means the chance to fish and perhaps to enjoy a delicious meal of fresh fillets. With nearly two thousand lakes to choose from, the angler in the group will likely go crazy with anticipation.

The major game fish species found in the canoe country are walleye, lake trout, northern pike, and smallmouth bass. A few lakes contain largemouth bass and panfish, and there are a handful of brook trout lakes. Those interested in what fish are to be found in which lake should consult my book *A Boundary Waters Fishing Guide,* which contains an index of lakes and fish species as well as chapters on the techniques and equipment needed to catch each species. See the Suggested Reading List.

Fishing season in Minnesota opens the Saturday nearest to May 15. Quetico lakes are open for lake trout fishing as soon as the ice departs (early to mid-May) and the general fishing season opener follows. Contact the Ontario Ministry of Natural Resources for further information. Of course you'll need to purchase the appropriate licenses before you wet your line.

The best fishing for lake trout is just after ice-out and again in autumn. Walleye fishing peaks in June but can be good throughout the entire summer. Smallmouth angling is tops in June through early July. Northern pike can be counted on to bite just about anytime, but the best fishing is in late August through September, when the truly big pike begin to lard up for the winter. Hold on to your rod!

Equipment should be kept to a bare minimum. A five-by-eight plastic tackle box will hold all the lures you'll need. Artificial baits are very effective: the best are spinners, jigs, spoons, and minnow-imitating plugs.

Although live bait may increase your success, it can be difficult to transport. You can't take minnows into the Quetico, although it is legal to do so in the BWCAW. Leeches are probably the best live bait for walleye, northern, and smallmouth and are the least difficult to transport and keep alive.

A light- to medium-action rod works best, and spinning tackle is the most versatile. With a quality reel and a good drag, anglers would be wise to stick with six- to eight-pound test premium monofilament fishing line. If you are a fly fisherman, consider fishing for smallmouth in June with mayfly imitations or deer hair poppers. It is fantastic. A landing net is largely unneeded and is just another thing to clutter up the canoe or lug across portages. Cord stringers work the best and are the most foolproof. Secure your rods to the gunwales of your canoe for transportation and protection. Never portage with a lure still attached to the line or it will eventually get caught on someone or something. The only other things you'll need are a needlenose pliers and a sharp fillet knife.

Practice catch-and-release angling. Keep only enough fish for your dinner, and carefully release the rest. Fish stored on a stringer do not fare well and often die and spoil or are consumed by snapping turtles, so trying to keep a mess to take home is foolish and ends up in waste.

Not only are smaller fish better tasting, but releasing the big ones ensures good natural reproduction since older fish spawn more successfully. Consider also that there is now (sadly) a health advisory for those consuming these wilderness fish. Mercury has been found in the flesh of fish in every lake that has been tested in the BWCAW and Quetico. Mercury poses serious health risks if consumed in large quantities, especially for small children, pregnant women, or women who intend to become pregnant. Up-to-date consumption guidelines will come with the Minnesota or Ontario fishing license. Be sure to read them.

As a rule of thumb, small fish contain less mercury and therefore are safer to eat because they have been a part of the food chain for a shorter time. If you consume just a few meals of fish during your visit you don't have much to worry about, unless you're one of the high-risk individuals just mentioned.

It is a good idea never to take your fish back to camp until they are filleted. Cleaning fish in camp attracts flies and bears and can leave a smelly mess. Paddle a few blocks away from camp and fillet your fish there. Dispose of fish remains by chopping them into fine pieces and leaving them on a shoreline rock for scavengers such as gulls. If scavengers don't clean them up before you leave the lake, return and bury the fish remains back in the woods in a shallow hole. Or you can do this in the first place. The key is to keep the smell and mess away from camp. And don't throw the guts in shallow water near camp. It takes weeks for it to break down, and meanwhile it taints every other camper's drinking water and looks terrible.

Reservations and Regulations for the Boundary Waters and Quetico

Both the Boundary Waters Canoe Area Wilderness and Quetico Provincial Park are managed wilderness areas. Those who visit overnight are required to have in their possession a valid travel permit. Each permit allows a group to enter from a specific entry point on a specific day—no variations. However, once you are in the wilderness you are free to travel as you wish.

If you will be entering both the Quetico and Boundary Waters, you'll need a separate permit for each, and when crossing the international border from the United States going into Canada, you'll have to stop at a Canadian customs office.

Day users to either area are not required to have a permit, unless you are using an outboard motor on one of the Boundary Waters' motorized lakes. Check with the U.S. Forest Service for further details regarding motorized travel within the wilderness. The motor ban applies to such things as generators, chain saws, and electric trolling motors—even to mechanized devices such as portage wheels (on all but a couple portages), carts, or bicycles.

The vast majority of visitors travel by paddle. Keep in mind that motors are allowed in only a few lakes in the Boundary Waters and are illegal throughout the Quetico. That doesn't mean you might not see a motorboat in the Quetico, however, because the guides from the La Croix Band of Ojibwa have special motor privileges on a few of the Quetico's lakes.

What is a permit?

As mentioned, a permit allows you to enter the Boundary Waters or Quetico; you need a different permit for each of the two wilderness areas. A permit is also a binding agreement between the party leader and the respective governing agency that you'll obey the regulations that protect the canoe country. As group leader, you are responsible for making each member of your party familiar with the rules and regulations, which come with each permit. A permit is not a reservation to camp at a particular campsite or on a particular lake. You may get to the destination of your dreams and find the sites all occupied. To camp in the Boundary Waters illegally is to damage the resource and risk a monetary fine or other punishment. Always be prepared to go farther than you planned to find a campsite.

Permits for both the Quetico and Boundary Waters can be reserved in advance, which is a wise idea if you have your heart set on a particular entry point. You can also take your chances and merely stop at a ranger station with the hope of obtaining a permit, something that is not unreasonable during early or late season. To be safe, however, reservations make sense.

Your permit is free, but both the U.S. Forest Service and Quetico Provincial Park officials will charge a small fee for making a reservation. There is no fee for camping on the U.S. side, but in the Quetico you'll be charged $3.00 (Canadian) per person nightly for each adult and half that amount for teens, with small children staying for free. You must pay this in advance. This amount is subject to change without notice.

To make a reservation for the Quetico, call (807) 597-2735 during business hours. You may charge your reservation and nightly fees to your Visa or Mastercard. Quetico permits must be picked up in person on the day of your entry during the hours between 8:00 A.M. and 5:00 P.M. at the ranger station nearest your entry point. These entry stations are located IN the wilderness, except French Lake, so getting your permit is not merely a matter of driving up to the door. Plan enough time to arrive during business hours. They are located on Saganaga, Basswood (Prairie Portage), Beaverhouse, Nym, Lac LaCroix, and French Lakes. Ontario fishing licenses are needed in Quetico and available at these ranger stations. These remote offices are staffed only from early or mid-May until mid-September.

Canadian customs

Remember that you must also clear Canadian customs when entering the Quetico. If you've driven to one of the northern entry points, you'll have already checked in at customs when entering Canada. If you enter from the south (BWCAW), you need to check in at either Sand Point, Saganaga, or Basswood (Prairie Portage) Custom Station. Only at Prairie Portage will you find customs located conveniently near the Quetico ranger station. At the other two plan on a day or two's travel between customs and the ranger station where you'll obtain your permit.

To obtain more information on Quetico's entry points and routes, contact the Ontario Ministry of Natural Resources, Quetico Provincial Park, Atikokan, Ontario, Canada P0T 1C0.

You can also use the phone and your credit card to make reservations for the Boundary Waters. Call the U.S. Forest Service's reservation office at (218) 720-5440. This number is for reservations only—no information regarding your route, the fishing, and so on is available at this number.

Boundary Waters permits also must be picked up in person by the designated group leader (or alternate). You may be asked to show proper identification. The permit should be picked up at the ranger station nearest your entry point, and can't be obtained any earlier than twenty-four hours before the departure date. Be prepared when visiting either the U.S. or Canadian ranger offices to spend some time receiving visitor instructions. This is also an excellent time to ask them any questions you have about your route, campsites, or recent reports of marauding black bears.

Reservations

You'll need to know your entry point and departure date choices before calling in your reservation, so spend some time planning before picking up the phone. Write to the U.S. Forest Service at P.O. Box 338, Duluth, MN 55801, or call (218) 720-5324, to request information on planning your trip to the Boundary Waters Canoe Area Wilderness.

Both the Quetico and Boundary Waters offices begin taking reservations on February 1 for the following season. Often the phone lines are jammed at this time, so be patient.

The Boundary Waters and Quetico have very similar rules; the only significant differences are that you must camp in a designated campsite in the BWCAW, but you may camp anywhere in the Quetico, and party size in the U.S. is limited to ten, but in the Quetico it is limited to nine. Remember that a BWCAW campsite must have both a permanently installed fire grate and a wilderness latrine to be a legal site.

Party sizes are restricted to the maximum number at all times. That means that even if you have two permits for your large group, you can't travel together, meet in campsites, or otherwise join up while in the Boundary Waters in groups larger than ten. Period.

Lots of folks try to abuse this regulation. Not only do they severely impact campsites and the visit of other campers, they stand to receive a hefty fine from the Forest Service. Quetico party size rules are similar. Always try to travel in groups of six or less. You'll find yourself traveling faster and seeing more wildlife, and locating a campsite suitable for your group size will be much easier. The majority of campsites just aren't suitable for large groups with lots of tents. By keeping your group small, you'll be helping to preserve the wilderness.

Other rules and restrictions

Containers of fuel, insect repellent, medicines, or personal toilet articles and other items that are not food or beverages are the only cans and bottles allowed in either the BWCAW or Quetico. Food or beverages must be packed in either a burnable container (paper, plastic bags, cardboard, etc.) or a hard container specifically designed for reuse (plastic camping bottles, Tupperware, etc.). In other words, no cans or glass bottles for food and beverages are allowed, and that includes deposit bottles such as those some soft drinks or beer come in.

All garbage must be packed out. Littering is illegal. Pick out unburned garbage, especially that noxious foil, from the fire grate before leaving. Keep an eye open for rubber bands, twist ties, and cigarette butts and pack them out.

In the Boundary Waters fires are allowed only in the steel fire grates at developed campsites. Quetico rules specify that you must build your fire on bare rock or bare mineral soil at least five feet from any flammable materials. It is illegal to leave a campfire unattended, so douse it each and every time you leave camp to go fishing or sightseeing, when you go to bed, and when you leave. Stir and soak the ashes repeatedly until they are cold to the touch.

Collect your firewood well away from camp and use only dead, downed wood. It is illegal to cut any type of live vegetation. Never strip birch bark from live trees. It is unsightly and can kill the tree. Plenty of birch bark can be found strewn over the forest floor. Don't cut down standing dead trees. They provide important wildlife habitat.

Both Ontario and Minnesota laws require a personal floatation device (PFD) for each person in the canoe. Minnesota requires that your canoe be licensed either in your home state or in Minnesota. If your home state doesn't require a license for canoes, you'll need to stop on your way to the BWCAW and obtain a Minnesota watercraft license. Unfortunately, these can be hard to obtain; they are not commonly sold over the counter at sporting good stores as are fishing licenses, but are available from county auditors or state offices. Contact the Minnesota Department of Natural Resources at (800) 652-9747.

Fishing licenses are required in both wilderness areas. Quetico rangers can issue a license at their ranger stations. Minnesota licenses are easily obtained at bait shops and other fishing and sporting stores. Call the toll-free number listed above for further information on Minnesota fishing licenses, prices, and seasons.

It is illegal to bring live bait fish, firearms, or fireworks into Quetico.

While these rules may seem like a lot to think about while on a wilderness trip, they are in place to protect the wilderness values for which you are visiting. Both the U.S. Forest Service and Quetico Provincial Park send teams of wilderness rangers into the field to make sure visitors are following these rules. Not only does failure to obey these laws harm the wilderness, it can result in a healthy fine or a visit before a magistrate. For the sake of the wilderness and other visitors to come, please practice no-trace camping techniques and follow the rules carefully.

Unfortunately an awful lot of boors visit the canoe country, and they care neither about the quality of your wilderness experience nor about preserving the wilderness. If you witness unlawful behavior, or come upon a campsite that has been trashed by slobs, report it to the nearest ranger station when you depart. The U.S. Forest Service has also established a hotline for reporting crimes in the Superior National Forest and BWCAW. You can leave an anonymous report seven days a week, twenty-four hours a day, by calling (800) 78CRIME.

Between budget cuts and small staffs, the twin wildernesses of the BWCAW and Quetico seldom see the number of rangers afield needed to truly cope with all the work of managing wilderness. Ultimately the responsibility for caring for it falls upon the shoulders of those of us who visit. Take pride in keeping a clean camp, obey the rules, and insist the other members of your group do so as well. It is your wilderness you're caring for.

Canoe Country Guardians

Two organizations have often stood alone in the struggle to protect the canoe country. Since the threats to the wilderness never cease, these groups can use your support.

Izaak Walton League of America
   1401 Wilson Boulevard, Level B
   Arlington, VA 22209

   The Izaak Walton League has been engaged in the canoe country's preservation since the 1920's. There would be not BWCAW without it. A national conservation group with thousands of active local chapters, it still serves as a watchdog for the BWCAW and Quetico.

Friends of the Boundary Waters Wilderness
   1313 Fifth Street SE, Suite 329
   Minneapolis, MN 55414

   Formed to fight for the Boundary Waters wilderness legislation passed in 1978, the Friends' sole purpose is to preserve and protect the ecosystem of the Quetico-Superior wilderness.

For More Information

BWCAW reservations:
   U.S. Forest Service
   (218) 720-5440

BWCAW information:
   U.S. Forest Service
   P.O. Box 338, Duluth, MN 55801
   (218) 720-5324

Quetico reservations, information,
   and Ontario fishing licenses:
   Ministry of Natural Resources
   Quetico Provincial Park
   108 Saturn Avenue
   Atikokan, Ontario   Canada P0T 1C0
   (807) 597-2735

Minnesota fishing and watercraft licenses:
   Minnesota Department of Natural Resources
   (800) 652-9747

Map sources for BWCAW and Quetico:
   W.A. Fisher Company
   Box 1107, Virginia, MN 55792

Creative Consultants McKenzie Maps
727 Board of Trade Building
Duluth, MN 55802

Outfitter Information:

Atikokan Chamber of Commerce
P.O. Box 997
Atikokan, Ontario, Canada P0T 1C0

Cook Chamber of Commerce
Cook, MN 55723

Crane Lake Commercial Club
Crane Lake, MN 55725

Ely Chamber of Commerce
1600 Sheridan Street
Ely, MN 55731

Tip of the Arrowhead Association
Grand Marais, MN 55604

Lutsen-Tofte Tourism Association
Box 115
Lutsen, MN 55612

Suggested Reading List

Perhaps no wilderness has been featured in print more often the the Boundary Waters and Quetico. The visitor can easily read not only about the canoe country's history and charm but also about its routes and fishing before planning a trip. The following is a suggested reading list to make you more familiar with this wonderful country.

Canoe routes and fishing information

Boundary Waters Canoe Area, by Robert Beymer. An excellent two volume guide to the canoe routes of the BWCAW. Published by Wilderness Press.

A Paddler's Guide to Quetico Provincial Park, by Robert Beymer. Published by the W.A. Fisher Co., this book introduces the reader to the varied routes of the Quetico.

A Boundary Waters Fishing Guide, by Michael Furtman. This complete guide book to fishing the canoe country contains a valuable index to the lakes of the BWCAW and Quetico, describes the fish found in each, and gives pertinent information on water depth, and fishing pressure. Chapters focus on equipment, lures, and techniques, on cleaning and cooking the fish, and on canoe country lore. Published by NorthWord Press, Box 1360, Minocqua, WI 54548 (800) 336-9800.

On the canoe country wilderness in General

Canoe Country, by Florence Jaques. An endearing tale of a
visit to the canoe country fifty years ago. Beautifully
illustrated by husband Francis Jaques. Published by
University of Minnesota Press.

The works of Sigurd Olson: No writer has captured the
mood of the canoe country better than master environ-
mentalist and wilderness philosopher, Sigurd Olson.
All of his numerous books are treasures and are published by Alfred Knopf Publishers.

A Season For Wilderness, by Michael Furtman. The account
of a three month stay in the BWCAW by Furtman and
his wife, Mary Jo, as they perform the duties of Wilderness Rangers and deal with the visitors, weather and
magic of the canoe country. NorthWord Press, Box
1360, Minocqua, WI 54548 (800) 336-5666.

The Boundary Waters Journal, A quarterly magazine de-
voted exclusively to the BWCAW, Quetico, and
Superior National Forest. Features in-depth articles
and color photography on wilderness recreation,
nature, and conservation. Published by Boundary
Waters Journal Publishing Co., 9396 Rocky Ledge
Road, Ely, MN 55371 (800) 548-7319.

Other fine books from  Pfeifer-Hamilton Publishers

CampSights
Sam Cook

Another delightful collection of essays and stories from the North Country. Sam offers insights into the subtleties of the natural world that all too often go unnoticed. Sam's first two books, *Up North* and *Quiet Magic*, are also available from Pfeifer-Hamilton Publishers.

Hardcover, 208 pages, $16.95

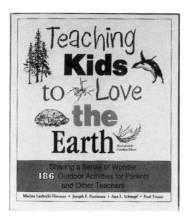

Teaching Kids to Love the Earth
Marina L. Herman, Ann Schimpf, Joseph Passineau, and Paul Treuer

A collection of 186 earth-caring activities designed for use with children of all ages to help them experience and appreciate the Earth. *Teaching Kids to Love the Earth* will enable you and the children you work with to experience a sense of wonder about the world we all share.

Softcover, 192 pages, $14.95

The North Shore:
A Four-Season Guide to Minnesota's Favorite Destination

Explore Minnesota's North Shore with this personal tour-guide. *The North Shore* will help you plan your adventures, from one-day excursions to two-week vacations. Read *The North Shore* as you plan your trip; then take it along to enjoy the milepost-by-milepost descriptions of Lake Superior's scenic splendor.

Softcover, 216 pages, $14.95

Canoe Country Wildlife:
A Field Guide to the Boundary Waters and Quetico
Mark Stensaas

Written for the "curious naturalist" in each of us, *Canoe Country Wildlife*, introduces you to the wildlife you are most likely to see as you travel in the North Woods. Filled with fascinating facts, handy checklists and suggested activities, it is a wonderful gift for anyone who enjoys the outdoors.

Softcover, 240 pages, $14.95

Gunflint: Reflections on the Trail
Justine Kerfoot

Justine Kerfoot has lived on Minnesota's remote Gunflint trail for five decades. She's gutsy and knowledgeable and humorous, most of all she's real—a unique woman of strength and character! Her keen observations and warm sensitivity recreate memorable episodes and touching moments from her years on the trail.

Hardcover, 208 pages, $16.95

Distant Fires
Scott Anderson

A classic canoe-trip story, with a twist of wry. Anderson's journey began on a front porch in Duluth, Minnesota and ended three months and 1,700 miles later at historic York Factory in Hudson Bay. The reader is treated to a breath of fresh northwoods air with every turn of the page.

Softcover, 176 pages, $12.95

To order write or call:

Pfeifer-Hamilton Publishers   Toll Free   800-247-6789
1702 E Jefferson   Fax   218-728-2631
Duluth MN 55812   Local   218-728-6807